CULTIVATING THE AFFLUENT II

LEVERAGING HIGH-NET-WORTH
CLIENT AND ADVISOR RELATIONSHIPS

Cultivating the Affluent II
Leveraging High-Net-Worth Client and Advisor Relationships
Copyright 1997 Institutional Investor, Inc. All rights reserved.

New York editorial and publishing offices:
488 Madison Avenue, 14th floor
New York, New York 10022
(212) 224-3300

The information contained herein is accurate to the best of the publisher's knowledge, however, the publisher can accept no responsibility for the accuracy or completeness of such information or for loss or damage caused by any use thereof.

Additional copies of this publication may be obtained by calling (212) 224-3800.

CULTIVATING THE AFFLUENT II

LEVERAGING HIGH-NET-WORTH
CLIENT AND ADVISOR RELATIONSHIPS

by
Russ Alan Prince and Karen Maru File

A publication of
Private Asset Management,
an Institutional Investor,Inc. newsletter

To

Sandi,

of course

Russ Alan Prince

To

Joe, Charlie and Mike

Karen Maru File

CULTIVATING THE AFFLUENT II

Leveraging High-Net-Worth Client and Advisor Relationships

Russ Alan Prince and Karen Maru File

Table of Contents

Introduction

Cultivating the Affluent (1995) explored a range of issues of vital importance to investment managers targeting the high-net-worth market: the goals and psychologies of affluent investors, the criteria they employ in selecting managers, their channels of information, as well as the steps investors go through in deciding to switch managers. The findings were based on surveys conducted by Prince & Associates at the request of *Private Asset Management*, a publication of **Institutional Investor, Inc.**; in shorter form the results of the surveys appeared in *PAM* in 1994 and 1995.

Probably the single most important lesson to emerge from the research was that success in the high-net-worth field does not hinge solely, or even most important, on impressive investment results. Every bit as vital is how a firm handles the "people" or "relationship" issues.

Second in importance only to client relationships is how investment managers get along with their wealthy clients' other advisors—attorneys, accountants, insurance agents and the like. The reason for this is that these other advisors provide a key source of referrals and therefore ensure a continuing stream of new business.

The interest greeting these findings prompted *PAM* to commission a new set of surveys by Prince and Associates. This research—also published in shorter form in *PAM*—charts in detail the elements underlying superior, business-building relationships, both with clients and with other advisors.

In the client portion of the study, a group of more than 400 wealthy investors were surveyed at regular intervals over a two-year period. This longitudinal aspect afforded a deeper insight into the behavior and desires of clients, as well as allowing the establishment of "baseline" estimates for such key matters as client mortality. The advisor portion of the study looks at the differences among lawyers, accountants and insurance agents, the advantages and disadvantages each group possesses from the vantage point of growing an investment management business, and the techniques to use in enlisting their cooperation.

We believe this material, presented here with detailed charts and tables, offers managers an invaluable tool in devising strategies to target the high-net-worth market.

Thanks go to Tom Lamont, Steve Murray and Chris Larson for their editorial efforts and to Michael Corsi, Dany Pena, Barbara Vogel, Nazneen Kanga, Dahlia Weinman and Chevaneese Hague for their work in producing and publishing the book.

Aimee Picchi
Managing Editor
Private Asset Management

PART I
GROWING YOUR BUSINESS THROUGH CLIENT RELATIONSHIPS

1

THE HIGH-NET-WORTH MARKET: FUNDAMENTALS

Investment managers dealing with the affluent aim to provide their clients with good investment performance and a high quality of service. That is their job and it is what clients expect. But, from a management firm's point of view, the goal is profitability. And how is profitability attained? By gathering assets.

There are various ways in which a firm can bring in more assets, but basically they boil down to two alternatives: raise more assets from existing clients or get more clients. Obviously, these are not exclusive. A successful firm will do both.

It might be thought that these two goals—persuading current clients to entrust more of their funds with your firm and enrolling new clients—require two separate strategies. To an extent, this is true. The activity of seeking out new clients can require initiatives that are out of place in dealing with existing clients. But to a surprising degree, the efforts and behaviors by managers that result in more funds from existing clients will also yield an added bonus of new clients.

One need not look far for the reason. In *Cultivating the Affluent*, we studied the channels of communication by which affluent investors learn of investment managers. The most important channel is other wealthy individuals, particularly satisfied clients of a firm. Referrals from highly satisfied clients is the golden road for growing your business. By the same token, unsatisfied clients are not merely at high risk of withdrawing their accounts, but they are extremely unlikely to give the referrals that drive growth.

19

In the first part of the book, we will examine in detail this all-important topic of client relationships, unpacking the elements of client satisfaction and charting a paradigm for building your business. In the second half we will discuss the different techniques for gaining referrals from advisors, particularly accountants, attorneys and insurance agents.

A Relationship Business?

We have asserted repeatedly that the quality of the interpersonal relationship between the affluent client and the investment manager is very often the driving force in the business of managing private wealth. This may seem too simple to require such repetition. Or it may seem open to another objection—it may seem, quite simply, wrong. Is it?

There is, after all, another answer to the question of what makes an investment manager successful. It is what we might call the face-value, or obvious, answer: to succeed in the investment management business, simply manage investments well. Make money for your clients and they'll give you more money to manage. New investors will flock to you when they hear of what you've done. Making money is paramount; nothing else really matters. Don't worry about being warm and fuzzy because the bottom line rules.

Admittedly, solid investment performance is a major determinant of money manager success. But to claim that investment performance constitutes the entire business, or even the greater part of it, is a fallacy. Were investment performance to be the sole or principal determining factor, then affluent investors would jump from one investment manager to another fairly frequently. But that does not happen.

Most high-net-worth clients instead view investment performance through the lens of the affluent investor/investment manager relationship. The stronger the relationship, the less attention clients pay to poor investment results. This situation can last for an extended period of time. *Cultivating the Affluent* spelled this lesson out in detail, at the same time identifying a number of strategic and tactical initiatives that enable managers to build their businesses by strengthening client relationships. "Improve client relationships" may sound like a simple and straightforward task, but in fact it requires managers to incorporate into their regular practice a host of specific behaviors.

Using these previous findings as a base, we undertook new research with the aim of arriving at an even fuller understanding of how to create relationships that bring in additional assets from existing clients as well as generate referrals. Studying the behavior and intentions of a sizable group of affluent investors over time offered the best way of attaining this understanding.

With this in mind, we undertook a study of more than 400 affluent investors. Each participant in the study had $500,000 or more in investable assets. We focused our attention on the investors' primary money managers, that is, the finance professional who managed the majority of an investor's assets. Investors were surveyed every six months for two consecutive years. This enabled us not only to evaluate the attitudes and psychology of the investors, but also to keep close track of their behavior.

One particular aspect of their behavior that we looked at very closely was the dismissal of a primary money manager. Investors who took this step were surveyed to determine their reasons for this action. Clearly, managers seeking to keep their clients need to understand as fully as possible the reasons investors have for leaving. In the remainder of this chapter, we will explore this topic.

Why High-Net-Worth Clients Leave

High-net-worth clients may discontinue their relationships with a money manager for a variety of reasons. In some cases it is death rather than dissatisfaction that severs the tie. Indeed, since high-net-worth clients are often middle-aged or elderly, their mortality rate is higher than that of groups with a more even age distribution. The current state of

Table 1.1

Analysis of Death			
End of Period	**2**	**3**	**4**
Number of HNW clients*	401	373	333
Number who died during the period	12	10	9
% death in a six-month period	2.9%	2.8%	2.7%
% deaths in a quarter	1.5%	1.9%	1.9%
Rate per 1,000 HNW clients per quarter	15	19	19

This number reflects the total number of HNW clients in the panel minus those who died during the period or who withdrew from study participation.

medical science does not allow even superior investment management to finesse death, but there are nevertheless some points to be made beyond asserting the fact of mortality.

First, we can look at the question of what death rate might be expected. Some of the investors participating in our research did unfortunately die during the course of the study. These events allowed us to create industry baseline data for client attrition due to death. In our sample, less than 3% of participating high-net-worth clients died in each of three six-month periods. The precise numbers appear in Table 1.1.

Our second point is that client assets do not necessarily leave because of client death. Actually, in most cases, assets remain put, especially if they are in trust. In other words, while death is inevitably part of the landscape, its consequences vary.

If we look at the details, certain patterns emerge. Of the 31 clients who died over the course of the study, 14 left the estate to a surviving spouse and 17 bequeathed it to children or other heirs. Of the 14 inheriting spouses, in eight cases trust arrangements locked the assets into particular investment managers and those assets did not move. In the six cases where a spouse inherited and was free to move assets, four spouses stayed with the money manager of record; two switched all the assets. This is a small sample, but still it is indicative: in cases where spouses inherit, they are likely to remain with the manager, thanks to shared decision-making and a mutual relationship built up over the years.

We see a different result when someone other than the spouse inherits and no trust legally binds the assets to the investment manager. Of the 17 cases where children or nonspouses inherited, 11 were not bound by trust. In every one of those 11 cases (100%), the assets were switched to a new manager.

This phenomenon we see again and again. Children want to use their own advisors. Many of the inheriting generation already have advisors that they themselves selected. They don't want Mommy and Daddy's advisors—they want their own. Most members of the inheriting generation are eager to put the assets to work with their own professionals.

To counteract this natural tendency, more and more investment managers have implemented programs to woo their clients' eventual heirs. These are fairly new departures, experimental in a sense. Some investment managers have sponsored "retreats" in which family wealth issues are discussed. Other money managers have concentrated efforts on designing highly focused educational material for the inheriting generation. The material furnishes useful information while also enhancing the position of the money manager with the younger generation.

Because these are relatively new techniques, it is not clear which approach works best. Still, it is a certainty that doing nothing is not a workable alternative—that path leads to the monies quickly exiting once the heirs have rights to it. And some of the current efforts have demonstrated their usefulness.

If children or nonspouses do inherit, the way for managers to feel secure about retaining assets is for those assets to be in trust. In our sample, in the six cases where trust arrangements existed, the assets did not move, for the reason that they could not be moved.

It is not surprising, therefore, that many investment management firms have either established trust companies, are in the process of doing so or at least considering the option. At a minimum, trusts represent a defensive strategy. When assets are not in trust, they move. Trusts prove invaluable in ensuring continuity of relationships with heirs.

Some firms, while recognizing the defensive virtues of the trust business, are now looking to trusts and estate planning as a proactive strategy for bringing new assets under management. Demographic trends, combined with the concern of many affluent investors to have comprehensive financial planning, mean that offering trust services can serve as an effective marketing tool for growing an investment management business.

We should emphasize that, while trust services have definitely proved their usefulness as a tool for managers seeking to grow their businesses, offering these services is not simply a matter of boning up on a few rules and regulations. Investment professionals who work with high-net-worth clients around estate issues need to acquire not only solid technical expertise but also a clear understanding of precisely where and how the estate planning and trust business intersects with the investment management business.

Death, of course, is not the only reason assets move between managers. Sometimes clients just decide they want to try a different manager. In other words, there is a certain degree of client turnover, or churn, in the industry. Of course, the fact that this turnover exists is well known, but we were curious about quantifying it. Our longitudinal research method enabled us to establish, we believe for the first time, what the industry average is by looking at a large number of clients serviced by a large number of investment managers.

It is only through research of this type that a well-founded industry-wide churn rate can be found. Some financial institutions do conduct surveys, but their results apply only to their own clients. Such research is informative, but does not enable managers to tell if they are doing better or worse than the industry as a whole. Similar objections apply to the surveys some investment managers do of their clients. In any case, the sample is usually too small to be representative. Moreover, one-shot cross-sectional studies do not last over ups and downs of a market, and so often provide misleading information. As we said, we believe that this longitudinal study offers the first published churn rate that can stand as an industry baseline, having been derived from a large sample of high-net-worth clients, employing enough different managers and over a long period of time.

How you use it will depend on you. For a start, you can compare your own churn rate with it. (We assume that you keep informed of how many clients you lose, on a quarterly and yearly basis. This is key information, and if you haven't kept an eye on it, you should start doing so now.) If, for example, you have 200 clients and two have left over the past quarter (transferring all assets to a new manager), are you doing well, or not?

You're doing well. As Table 1.2 shows, the industry baseline churn rate is 2.2%, about twice your rate in the example. The industry as a whole loses 8.8% of its high-net-worth clients per year.

Over the course of the study, 52 clients left their managers. Why? Was it because of inadequate investment performance? Or was it because of poor interpersonal relationships between client and manager? Or did both factors contribute?

We found that it was quite rare for an investment manager to fail a client on both investment performance and relationship grounds. In general, the problem lay in one area or the other. Our findings from this latest survey confirmed the observations we had made in *Cultivating the Affluent* on the reasons that affluent investors switch money managers.

As we said, 52 of the affluent investors in our survey left their man-

Table 1.2

Client Defection "Churn" Rate			
End of Period	**2**	**3**	**4**
Number of HNW clients*	401	373	333
Number who defected during the period	16	30	6
% defections in a six-month period	3.8%	8.0%	1.8%
% defections in a quarter	1.9%	4.0%	0.9%
Rate per 1,000 HNW clients per quarter	19	40	9

This number reflects the total number of HNW clients in the panel minus those who died during the period or who withdrew from study participation.

agers. For the great majority—45 of the 52—the reason for leaving was a failure in the relationship. Seven out of the 52 fired their managers because of dissatisfaction over fundamentals or investment performance.

We queried the investors who switched regarding their perceptions of the fired managers on a number of issues. The two charts below—one for those who left because of poor investment performance [Chart 1.3], the other for relationship failures [Chart 1.4]—spell out their responses. The first chart makes it clear that results, not relational nuances, mattered for those who left because of investment performance.

Chart 1.3

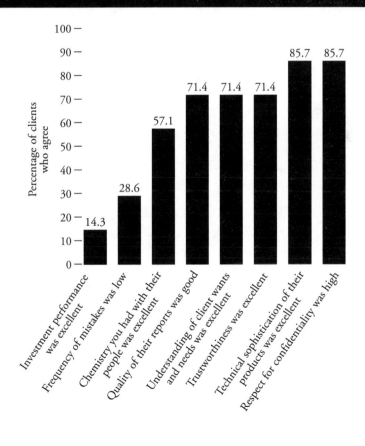

Base is seven people who defected principally because of poor investment performance.

It is worth noting that both groups of investors, even though they decided to switch managers, tended to be satisfied with the quality of the reports provided by their advisors as well as with the technical sophistication of their products. We find repeatedly that affluent investors do not make significant decisions—such as leaving a manager or adding assets—based on these issues.

Moving now from the reasons that prompt investors to switch managers to the monetary impact of such actions, it is clear that this impact is considerable. When affluent clients leave a manager, they move sub-

Chart 1.4

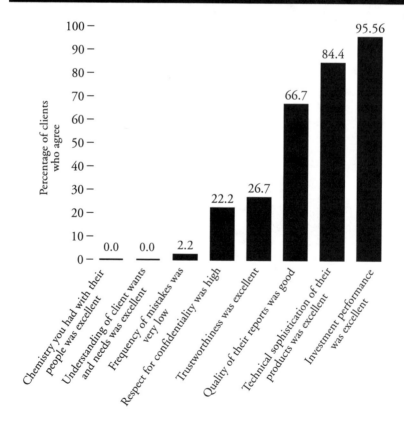

Table 1.5

Amount of Assets Moved

Assets transferred	Investment results group*	Poor relationship group**
$500K to $1M	28.6%	17.8%
$1M to $3M	14.3%	22.2%
$3M to $5M	28.6%	51.1%
$5M or more	28.6%	8.9%

* Base is seven investors.
** Base is 45 investors.

stantial assets. In Table 1.5 we show the amount of assets moved, breaking it down by those who left on grounds of investment performance and those who left for relationship reasons.

In the scale of assets transferred, the results perhaps do not justify drawing a distinction between our two groups of dissatisfied clients. However, we do see a difference between the groups when we look at the number of new firms used [Table 1.6]. Investors who fire a manager over

Table 1.6

Number of New Firms Used

Number of new firms	Investment results group*	Poor relationship group**
One	85.7%	37.8%
Two	14.3%	44.4%
Three	0.0%	8.9%
Four	0.0%	8.9%

* Base is seven investors.
** Base is 45 investors.

Table 1.7

Experience Factors in New Firm Choice

New home of transferred assets	Investment results group*	Poor relationship group**
Firms with which the client had previously invested	87.1%	78.6%
Firms with which the client had never previously invested	0.0%	1.4%
Both	12.9%	20.0%

* Base is seven investors.
** Base is 45 investors.

investment performance tend to concentrate their assets with just one new firm; those who leave because of relationship problems are more likely to use two or more new firms.

We will close this chapter with a point worth emphasizing: when affluent investors switch firms, they choose to concentrate their assets with money managers with whom they have had experience [Table 1.7]. This tendency shows most strongly among the investors who left because of poor investment performance, but it was quite noticeable among the relationship-failure group as well.

Clearly, managers should bear in mind this preference that clients have for working with managers they already know; it means that the opportunity often exists to enhance a relationship with an existing client. *Cultivating the Affluent II* offers a detailed look at the switching behavior of affluent clients and the openings this process offers to astute managers.

2

THE BUSINESS BUILDING PARADIGM

In this chapter we want to emphasize and document the importance of keeping clients satisfied. Highly satisfied, we should say, because in the end that is what matters for building a business. Clients who are highly satisfied increase their own accounts with their investment managers and refer their friends and associates.

We are aware that this constant harping on client satisfaction may sound like a broken record—a steady repetition of a particularly obvious point. Of course, clients must be treated well—whoever would think otherwise?

Unfortunately, the answer to this query: a fair number of investment managers, judging by the high levels of dissatisfaction we keep picking up in our surveys. While perfectly ready to grant the importance of client satisfaction, many managers seem to think satisfaction follows automatically from good investment performance. For most clients, it doesn't.

Drawing on the findings of this longitudinal study and other research, we have developed an approach—we call it the Business Building Paradigm—for growing an investment management business by leveraging existing relationships with high-net-worth clients.

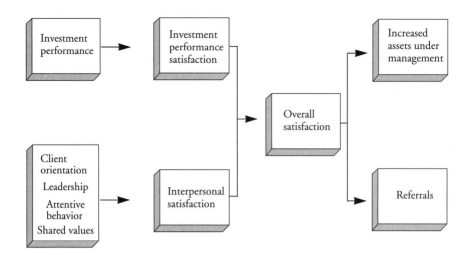

Business Building Paradigm

In this visual display we have placed client satisfaction at the center of the process. Psychologically, the determining variable in building an investment management business is client satisfaction. In a nutshell, the more completely satisfied the affluent client is with the manager, the more assets the client will entrust to the manager and the more referrals the client will make.

This matter of additional assets is the first benefit of satisfaction. We know that, in general, high-net-worth clients prefer to use multiple money managers. They don't want all their investable assets to be tied up with one firm. Using two or more firms gives the investor a range of advice and access to different packages of products, as well as diversifying risk.

But you, as an investment manager, have a different end in view. Your goal is to obtain as great a "share of customer" as possible. Satisfaction is the road to achieving this objective, to becoming the "go-to" manager. Also, affluent investors look to each other for information on money managers. Every satisfied client should be seen as a gateway to other affluent investors. While steps need to be taken to obtain referrals from satisfied clients, it should be clear that those steps will pay a dividend only if the client is satisfied.

In the next few chapters we will look at the components of the Business Building Paradigm, focusing in turn on investment performance, client orientation, leadership, attentive behavior and shared values. But first we want to give some quantitative support to our claims about satisfaction.

To start with, we have said that our surveys have picked up a significant measure of client dissatisfaction. What exactly does this mean? A senior officer of a national investment management firm once said, "If affluent clients are unhappy, they will leave. As long as they're not leaving, I know they're not unhappy."

This quotation would seem to suggest that clients are generally satisfied. We know there is a certain amount of client turnover or "churn" in the industry, but few people would claim that great hordes of clients are shifting firms all the time. Does this mean they are basically satisfied?

Not according to our surveys. We looked specifically at 1) satisfaction with investment performance and 2) satisfaction with the quality of the interpersonal relationship. Overall satisfaction blends these two components.

Chart 2.1

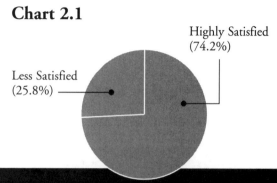

Less Satisfied
(25.8%)

Highly Satisfied
(74.2%)

Investment Performance Satisfaction

We found that while the majority—about three-quarters—of our sample of affluent investors declared themselves highly satisfied with their firm's investment performance, a much smaller number—less than one-third—were highly satisfied with the quality of the interpersonal relationship they have with their money managers. Apparently, investment managers are doing a good job running the money, but not such a good job running the relationships. This data comes from a period when the markets were generally rising. It may bode ill for complacent managers when the markets take another turn.

The specific percentages we found were as follows: for investment performance, 74.2% of those surveyed were highly satisfied [Chart 2.1], and 25.8% less satisfied; for quality of the interpersonal relationship, 28.6% were highly satisfied, and 71.4% were less satisfied [Chart 2.2].

Chart 2.2

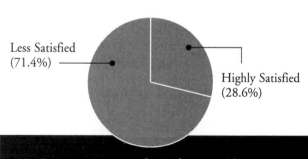

Less Satisfied
(71.4%)

Highly Satisfied
(28.6%)

Interpersonal Relationship Satisfaction

As we mentioned, overall satisfaction arises out of positive feelings regarding both investment perfor-

Chart 2.3

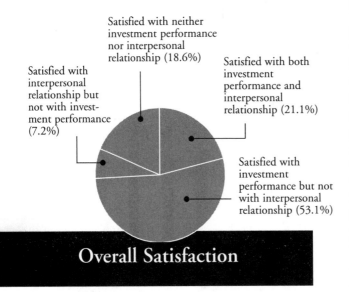

Satisfied with neither investment performance nor interpersonal relationship (18.6%)

Satisfied with interpersonal relationship but not with investment performance (7.2%)

Satisfied with both investment performance and interpersonal relationship (21.1%)

Satisfied with investment performance but not with interpersonal relationship (53.1%)

Overall Satisfaction

mance and the interpersonal relationship. When we look at our group of investors with this in mind, we find that only just more than one-fifth (21.1%) were highly satisfied on both grounds [Chart 2.3]. About half (53.1%) were highly satisfied with investment performance but less satisfied with their interpersonal relationships with their money managers. A small number (7.2%) were highly satisfied on relationship grounds but not with investment performance. A little less than one-fifth (18.6%) were satisfied with neither. It is likely that this last group will, if this situation continues, shift its assets to another manager.

The payoff of satisfaction is increased assets from clients themselves and new client referrals. We have said this before, but in this survey we were able to quantify these benefits. Specifically, for our sample of 318

Table 2.4

Satisfaction Levels*—Increasing Assets Under Management

	Investment performance satisfaction	
Interpersonal relationship satisfaction	Less satisfied	Highly satisfied
Less satisfied	0.0%	11.8%
Highly satisfied	9.6%	24.2%

*Based on survey of 318 affluent investors.

affluent investors, we have correlated satisfaction levels with average transfers of new assets and with clients' self-assessed likelihood of making a referral in the next six months.

We found that affluent clients who are highly satisfied with investment performance (but not delighted with their interpersonal relationships with investment managers) will transfer an average of 11.8% additional assets to the investment manager [Table 2.4]. (That is, a client with a $1 million account with a money manager would add $118,000 to his or her portfolio, in this satisfaction scenario.) On the other hand, clients highly satisfied with the interpersonal relationship but not with investment performance were also likely to add funds to their accounts, but in slightly smaller amounts—an average transfer of new funds equivalent to 9.6% of assets under management.

Naturally enough, clients satisfied with both investment performance and their interpersonal relationship added funds in the greatest proportion. These clients, our survey found, will add funds to augment their portfolios by 24.2% on average. By the same token, affluent investors satisfied in neither area were not inclined to increase their accounts at all— their average increase was 0.0%.

When we look at the impact of satisfaction on the likelihood of an affluent investor making a referral, we see a somewhat-altered picture. Once again, investors satisfied in neither the investment performance nor the relationship areas were not likely to take the desired actions: these investors said there was no likelihood of their making a referral [Table 2.5]. And investors satisfied in both areas were most likely to make referrals; on a 10-point scale, they gave themselves an 8.7 probability of refer-

Table 2.5

Satisfaction Levels*—Likelihood of New Referrals		
	Investment performance satisfaction	
Interpersonal relationship satisfaction	Less satisfied	Highly satisfied
Less satisfied	0.0	3.7
Highly satisfied	6.8	8.7

*Based on survey of 318 affluent investors.

ring new clients within the next six months.

It is when we attend to clients who are highly satisfied in one area but not the other—either investment performance or the interpersonal relationship—that we see a pattern somewhat at variance with that for increasing assets. Both groups of clients are somewhat likely to make referrals, but those highly satisfied with the interpersonal relationship are significantly more so. Investors who are happy about their relationships (but not especially with the investment performance) gave themselves a 6.8 likelihood (on a 10-point scale) of making referrals within the next six months; investors highly satisfied with the performance of their investments but not with their relationship put this probability at 3.7.

These findings demonstrate how vital it is for building a business to achieve high levels of client satisfaction. It should be clear that either kind of satisfaction—investment performance or interpersonal—can produce positive business results. Obviously, the goal should be to produce both kinds.

In our Business Building Paradigm, we identified the ingredients that produce satisfaction. They are:

- Investment performance
- Client orientation
- Leadership
- Attentive behavior
- Shared values

As an aid to memory, we will refer to these as I-CLAS. The hyphen signals the distinction between investment performance, on the one hand, and the four elements or factors contributing to quality relationships.

The I-CLAS methodology emphasizes relationship management (with four components) compared to investment performance (with one component). There are reasons for this. One is that we found, in our longitudinal survey, that six times as many clients defected because of a poor relationship with their money manager as left because of poor investment performance.

Another reason has to do with differentiating yourself in a competitive market. Yes, solid investment performance is not only important, it is vital. But many investment management firms can (or claim they can) provide sound investment performance. What manager is going to promise substandard investment performance? Competence in this area may be seen as a given, on many occasions. Quality of client service can make a money manager stand out. So few managers provide truly great customer service that it is relatively easy to excel in this area.

In the following chapters we will examine each element of the I-CLAS system in detail, beginning with investment performance. Our emphasis on relationship issues should not, in any way, suggest that this key area can be ignored.

3

INVESTMENT PERFORMANCE

Investment performance is unquestionably important. No matter how good a job a money manager does at relationship management, inferior investment performance will eventually torpedo the relationship. The affluent client will leave—and leave poorer for the experience.

Having said this, we must go on to note that the issue is not investment performance in the abstract or according to some universal criterion, but rather the client's satisfaction with investment performance. Stellar investment performance as measured by industry benchmarks is not necessarily the same thing as satisfaction with investment performance. Often, in fact, there is no correlation between satisfaction—a very subjective matter—and outstanding performance according to generally agreed-upon standards.

What matters is the client's perception. The key here is that the standard the client uses can be heavily influenced by the actions of the money manager. While there are accepted market indices, these need not be the standards used by high-net-worth clients. Investment managers who excel in growing their business generally do a good job of managing their clients' expectations as well as managing their monies. To use language a bit more euphemistic, what managers need to do is educate their clients and so play an important part in defining the standards the client uses for judging the manager's performance.

Naturally, there are limits to what even the most adroit management of expectations can achieve. Investors are never happy about losing money.

When a manager does indeed lose significant amounts of money, it is often hard to work around the situation.

Still, intelligent management of expectations can achieve a great deal. Even when an investment portfolio has fared quite poorly, affluent clients may, if handled well, remain satisfied. An example may make this seeming implausibility more understandable.

The case we have in mind is that of a leading money management firm that specializes in value investing. This firm goes to great pains to educate clients on the logic of value investing. When a client's portfolio has done poorly, the situation is explained as a matter of the market not having recognized the intrinsic value of the securities selected. To take advantage of this insight, the client is urged to entrust even more money to the firm, to obtain more of the undervalued securities. Historically, this money manager has been successful in obtaining more assets even when investment performance, by generally accepted measures, rated as substandard. The manager has also obtained referrals from clients despite this lackluster performance. Interestingly, this management of expectations has worked with institutional clients as well as high-net-worth individuals.

The theme in this management of expectations is concentration on investment management style, as opposed to investment performance. This means that when performance is poor, attention is directed to how the money is managed, not to the end result.

This case agrees with findings in *Cultivating the Affluent* that wealthy investors attach great importance to investment management style. We found (in a survey of 847 affluent investors) that 84.1% saw investment management style as of great importance in the selection of a money manager; by contrast, only 26.6% considered the manager's performance track record as very important.

In emphasizing management style as a tool for managing expectations, we are not saying that managers should necessarily preach value or growth, or equity small-cap compared to equity large-cap. Investment management style is how money is managed. For instance, we might consider a manager of managers program. What would be the investment management style in this instance? In such a scenario, investment management style would translate to the ability to match a high-net-worth individual's investment needs with the appropriate money manager(s). In other words, investment management style needs to be conceptualized broadly to embrace what the money manager is offering.

The process of managing expectations should begin when a money manager first introduces his/her services to affluent prospects. A helpful step, often taken with institutional clients but less commonly with affluent individuals, is the formulation of an investment plan. (For example, in a survey of 3,724 physicians, it turned out that only 15.8% had a formal detailed strategy for investing. Source: *Physician Financial Planning in a Changing Environment*, McGraw-Hill 1996.)

An investment plan can prove useful in itself. Beyond that, the underlying logic of such an approach often helps in managing clients' expectations. Basically, the argument for an investment plan centers on the fact that too few people approach investing in an organized fashion. We have found four main reasons that investment plans prove helpful and attractive to affluent clients. They are:

1. Recognizing uniqueness. The issue here is that of creating an investment portfolio customized to the unique needs of each high-net-worth client.

2. Ensuring risks are acceptable. This ensures that affluent clients are aware of the potential volatility of their investment portfolios and are comfortable with the level of risk chosen.

3. Enabling comparisons to appropriate benchmarks. The manager can help set investment objectives and educate the affluent investor regarding benchmarks that are realistic.

4. Taking emotion out of the process. Emotions often result in knee-jerk reactions. A well-formulated investment plan can help the money manager keep the attention of the affluent investor and so help keep the assets of the investor even when some hot investment looks alluring or when performance is substandard.

All in all, an investment plan can help an investor meet his/her goals and at the same time assist the finance professional in managing client expectations. The most effective plans incorporate four components. These are:

1. Statement of objectives. Why is the affluent individual investing? The goals that he or she is trying to reach need to be spelled out.

2. Risk tolerance. As indicated above, risk is a potent issue for investors. The plan should address this, specifying the level of risk the affluent investor is willing to accept.

3. Amount to be invested. Taking into account the two previous components—investment goals and level of acceptable risk—the plan should state how much money needs to be invested.

4. Benchmarks. Recurring to what was said above, the manager and investor should agree on what constitutes success. This will enable the affluent client to know if the plan is working.

Drawn up in this way, an investment plan can serve as a powerful tool in managing the expectations of affluent investors. In the real world it is difficult or impossible to deliver stellar investment performance quarter after quarter after quarter, so management of expectations must play an important role in business success.

Generally speaking, satisfaction with investment performance stems from a manager meeting or exceeding an agreed-to benchmark. Doing a respectable job of running the money, combined with appropriately managing clients' expectations, should usually produce this result. Given that 74.2% of the affluent investors surveyed in our study declared themselves highly satisfied with their investment performance, we can conclude that either the money managers in question did a truly exceptional job of managing portfolios over the two-year study, or they did a good job of running the money and at the same time did a good job of managing expectations. In most cases, we believe, it was probably the latter.

We now shift our focus to the techniques and orientations of management necessary to build strong client relationships. In the next chapter we will discuss client orientation.

4

CLIENT
ORIENTATION

Client orientation is one of the buzz terms in the high-net-worth field. Managers talk frequently about how they are client-oriented, yet the term is rarely defined. In this chapter we will look at the behaviors and attitudes that make up a client-oriented approach. We will also see how they correlate with client satisfaction.

We looked to high-net-worth clients themselves to define this term for us. Clients say they know their managers are client-oriented when they ask a lot of questions, feel them out about their needs and seem eager to communicate with them. After talking to many clients, we came to conclude that client-centeredness involves three major components. They are:

- Aggressive time management,
- Addressing client needs thoroughly and
- Fostering client involvement and participation.

Let's look at each of these components in detail.

Affluent clients view aggressive time management as a key sign that their money managers are client-oriented. Basically, it is a matter of the managers demonstrating in their behavior that they consider the client's time to be valuable, that clients need to be kept scrupulously current and that they put the client's need for prompt service above all else.

The great majority—more than three-quarters—of clients who are highly satisfied with their interpersonal relationships with their investment managers say that their managers perform well in these areas. But a much smaller proportion of less-satisfied clients give their managers good marks. In Table 4.1 we show exactly how clients responded to

Table 4.1

Time Management and Interpersonal Satisfaction

	Less satisfied	Highly satisfied
Manager takes the greatest pain to be punctual	49.0%	76.8%
Services client's needs faster than other top professionals	40.4%	81.2%
Goes to lengths to be sure client is always up to date with the relevant information	50.3%	88.3%
Keeps client posted on new developments or information that concerns investments	31.7%	79.9%

these assessments of their money managers on time-management issues.

Clearly, there is a significant connection between aggressive time management and client satisfaction. It is perhaps surprising that managers do not make greater efforts in this area, given that such a simple matter (for example) as punctuality can pay big dividends in satisfaction.

But there is more to client orientation than managing time. The second major component is that of addressing client needs thoroughly. Affluent clients feel "cared about" when managers show interest in their individual circumstances and concerns, and encourage them to talk about their hopes and goals. High-net-worth investors prefer managers to listen, not explain.

In studying this area, we asked our survey participants whether or not they agreed with a number of characterizations of their money managers—did the manager make a major effort to understand the client's needs? Did the manager listen carefully to questions and work closely with the client in defining needs? Did the manager provide services that were customized and tailored to the client's needs? Strikingly, those clients who were highly satisfied with their relationships virtually unanimously rated their managers positively in these areas. (For a number of the specific queries, they were unanimous.) Clients who were less satisfied with their personal relationships were much less likely to say these descriptions fit their managers. Table 4.2 shows exactly what we asked, and what percentages of clients responded positively.

Table 4.2

Client Needs Orientation and Interpersonal Satisfaction

	Less satisfied	Highly satisfied
Manager makes an exceptional effort to understand client's unique needs	32.7%	100.0%
Works closely with client to define needs in considerable detail	32.7%	100.0%
Listens carefully to questions in order to understand fully client's needs	39.4%	100.0%
Is extremely responsive to client's needs	35.3%	100.0%
Provides services that were customized to client's needs	73.9%	98.8%
Provides very tailored services and solutions to client's needs	71.4%	96.1%

When it was a question of providing individualized services to clients, a substantial majority of the "less-satisfied" group of clients rated their managers well. Clearly, providing customized services is the nature of the investment management industry for high-net-worth clients, so the prevalence of good ratings here is not surprising. But on the queries that had to do with listening and attending to the client's needs, only about one-third of the "less-satisfied" group saw their managers in a positive light. We could hardly look for more conclusive evidence that managers need to listen to, as opposed to lecture, their affluent clients.

The third component of client-orientation is that of fostering client participation and involvement. This is one of the simplest and most effective, but also most frequently overlooked, ways of creating greater satisfaction among affluent clients. Previous research has shown that not only does this kind of involvement quite often lead to the client adding assets and making referrals, it is also one of the most significant reasons the money manager will not be sued.

The differences in this area between highly satisfied clients and less-satisfied ones are remarkable [Table 4.3]. We looked at a range of ways in which managers can encourage client participation, such as encouraging

Table 4.3

Fostering Client Involvement and Interpersonal Satisfaction

	Less satisfied	Highly satisfied
Manager encourages client to ask questions freely about services being provided	11.3%	100.0%
Willing to meet with client as often as client feels necessary	38.7%	95.0%
Willing to take as long as necessary to explain services to client	25.2%	93.8%
Very careful to solicit client's preferences about what client needs to discuss	0.0%	86.3%
Encourages client to be very active in expressing opinions at meetings	2.9%	83.8%
Careful to solicit client's preferences on number of times to meet	13.4%	67.5%
Provides client with very well thought out alternatives suited to client's unique needs	6.3%	93.8%

the client to ask questions, being willing to take as much time as necessary to explain services, soliciting the client's views about what should be discussed and frequency of meetings, as well as (on a less-procedural plane) giving the client investment alternatives, all particularized to the client's needs. The great majority of highly satisfied clients said their money managers did these things; with less-satisfied clients, only a minority (usually small, and in one case nonexistent) attributed these behaviors to their money managers.

Perhaps, we should add a word regarding the offering of investment choices to the client. Nearly all (93.8%) of the highly satisfied clients said their managers gave them a choice of investment alternatives, each of the alternatives suited their unique needs. By way of contrast, less than 10% of the less-satisfied group of clients said this happened. In most cases, in the field of investments there is no one absolutely right answer. To show a client a number of "right" answers can make the manager appear more client-oriented. In some cases, managers can dramatically improve their relationships with clients by providing a range of alternatives; getting the client involved in the decision-making process usually enhances the quality of the interpersonal relationship. Moreover, it is a "no-lose" situation for the investment manager. Often, high-net-worth clients who get involved in the final decision of how to invest their funds are happier both with the investment decision and with the decision to employ that particular money manager.

As we have said, client orientation involves three major components: aggressive time management, addressing client needs thoroughly and fostering client involvement. Performing well in these areas will have a major impact on client feelings of satisfaction.

5

LEADERSHIP

One advantage of being affluent is that you can buy the best. Certainly, high-net-worth clients feel this way with regard to the professional services they retain. In particular, when it comes to managing their money, affluent clients want to feel confident that they are working with leaders in the field. And having made a hiring choice, affluent investors like to receive confirmation that their choice is a good one. In this chapter we will look at the forms this confirmation can take. We will examine the elements of leadership and the concrete ways in which investment managers can demonstrate their leadership in the profession, thereby reinforcing their clients' sense of good judgment in selecting them and creating a high degree of satisfaction.

We should point out that, from the viewpoint of a high-net-worth client, leadership in the field does not necessarily equate with having the largest investment management firm as measured by personnel or assets under management. Nor does it necessarily refer to firms that might be famous for providing financial services to pension funds or other institutional clients. High-net-worth clients want advisors who are leaders in the field of money management for affluent investors like themselves.

It is also vital to bear in mind that we are talking about an extremely fragmented market. No investment manager enjoys a dominant presence. There are thousands of small boutique money managers and also financial planners engaged in managing assets for wealthy clients.

It is quite possible for each and every one of

these advisors, as well as for the larger firms, to be seen by their high-net-worth clients as industry leaders.

We see leadership as made up of three related virtues:

- Technical prowess;
- Emphasis on quality; and a
- Passion for service.

To achieve the highest satisfaction ratings from their affluent clients, investment managers must excel in all three areas.

The importance affluent clients attach to technical prowess is perhaps easiest to understand. Affluent clients select their investment managers with great care, collecting many endorsements before making a choice and often testing a new manager with a "trial period" involving a limited volume of assets. Clients need reassurance that their investment manager is one of the "best in the class."

We canvassed our sample of high-net-worth investors by offering them a number of positive statements regarding the technical prowess of their managers, and asking whether or not they agreed with these characterizations [Table 5.1]. Not surprisingly, we found that clients who are highly satisfied with their interpersonal relationships with their managers are considerably more likely to see their managers as technically expert. Half or more of even those clients who are less satisfied with their interpersonal relationships viewed their managers positively in this area. Most managers are doubtless technically expert in investments compared to most investors, and perhaps this accounts for these positive results. Still,

Table 5.1

Technical Prowess and Interpersonal Satisfaction

	Less satisfied	Highly satisfied
Manager is extremely knowledgeable about business even compared to those considered top in the field	68.3%	82.1%
Conducts work according to the highest possible standards	57.0%	74.8%
Is a top expert in the investment field	64.4%	71.3%
Is extremely experienced in investments	51.7%	66.3%

a significant number of investors—even investors who are highly satisfied in general with their interpersonal relationships—did not consider their managers as exemplars of technical prowess. Clearly, there is still some room at the top, and money managers can do a better job of communicating their technical prowess.

What can managers do to reinforce their clients' perceptions of their technical expertise? A good number of investment managers have found answers to this question. One approach is to send out press clippings of speaking engagements by the staff of the firm. Often this is done for almost any function, since it is not only the nature of the audience but also the number of times the staff members have been asked to speak that matter. Remember that positive perceptions need to be reinforced whenever possible; this technique is not effective when it is used once and then forgotten.

Another useful technique is the concise but pointed testimonial to the technical expertise of the managers. Clearly, the use of testimonials needs to be managed carefully to ensure client confidentiality. Efforts to enhance understanding of the manager's investment style can also bolster a sense of the manager's expertise. This kind of educational process helps the firm to manage client expectations, a key part of producing client satisfaction.

The second ingredient of leadership is an emphasis on quality. When we speak of quality, what we have in mind is providing precisely the service promised, reliability, perfectionism and putting the interests of the

Table 5.2

Quality Orientation and Interpersonal Satisfaction

	Less satisfied	Highly satisfied
Manager has always provided precisely the service promised	35.6%	48.3%
Is exceptionally reliable	37.7%	52.3%
Puts client's interest above his/her own	24.2%	53.8%
Is more of a perfectionist than other top professionals	11.9%	24.5%

client above those of the manager. When we asked our survey sample what they thought of their managers in these areas, we found a great deal of room for improvement [Table 5.2]. As usual, the highly satisfied group of clients rated their managers more positively than did the less-satisfied group, but half or more of the investors still did not see their money managers as displaying these hallmarks of a fixation on quality.

What do managers need to do to improve this situation? They can start by communicating to clients their commitment to perfectionism, to unfailing reliability and to delivering on all promises. Both verbal and written statements can be used. But these statements will backfire, in terms of satisfaction, unless managers do actually live up to their promises.

A passion for service is the third element we identified as making up quality leadership. What leadership means here is an attention to issues that affect client satisfaction and an aggressive effort to deliver on these matters. In particular, client satisfaction often hinges on how well managers handle complaints, anticipate concerns and react to client requirements.

Generally speaking, the managers whose clients are highly satisfied

Table 5.3

	Services Orientation and Interpersonal Satisfaction	

	Less satisfied	Highly satisfied
Manager deals with client concerns and complaints in the most timely manner possible	37.3%	86.3%
Takes reponsibility for any errors he/she makes	24.4%	62.8%
Encourages clients to discuss complaints and concerns	16.7%	53.8%
Responds to a service failure as an opportunity to provide great service	1.2%	27.5%
Encourages clients to provide manager with suggestions on how to improve operations and service	0.0%	13.8%

with their interpersonal relationships do well in these areas. They do less well when it comes to transforming a service failure into an opportunity to provide great service or soliciting thoughts from clients on how to improve operations and service. The managers who do not get great ratings in terms of interpersonal satisfaction do not fare particularly well in any of these assessments of leadership-quality service [Table 5.3].

Perhaps the most striking number in this chart is the 0.0% that turned up when we asked the less-satisfied group of clients if their managers actively solicit from them suggestions of what can be done to improve operations and service. Even among the highly satisfied group of clients, only 13.8% said their managers took this step. Asking clients about this, and also asking them if they have any concerns or complaints (apparently done by only half of the managers of the highly satisfied group of clients, and by less than one-fifth of the managers for the less-satisfied group), is a simple but effective way of demonstrating a commitment to service.

Showing sensitivity to client problems and concerns also sets a manager apart from those in the industry—all too many, unfortunately—who tend to assume that if a high-net-worth client does not bring a problem to the attention of the manager, then there isn't a problem. Often, money managers learn there are problems only when the client has already left. Given that only 28.6% of the clients in our study described themselves as being highly satisfied with the quality of their interpersonal relationship with their money manager, the odds are good that many money managers have less-than-fully satisfied clients. Taking a proactive attitude toward seeking out client concerns demonstrates leadership and will help build a manager's business.

6

ATTENTIVE
BEHAVIOR

We have isolated attentive behavior as a key element in producing interpersonal satisfaction for high-net-worth clients. Indeed, hand-holding (as we might also call it) is a prime component of this business.

When we look closely, we find that the vital factor here is not just being in contact with the client; perhaps even more important is who initiates contact. By and large, highly satisfied clients rarely call their investment managers; the managers take that crucial first step. Less-satisfied clients, on the other hand, often take the initiative in making contact, and in doing so they are frequently signaling their dissatisfaction.

One major reason for studying the relationship between the number and origin of contacts and the level of client satisfaction is that this factor is completely under the control of an investment manager. It is not hard to make a call to update an investor on his/her account; if doing this will keep clients happy, it is high time for managers to be aware of this fact. Such qualities as professionalism, empathy and technical prowess may seem "soft" or subjective (although we have outlined a number of specific ingredients and/or behaviors identified with them); the number of telephone calls a manager makes is hardly open to this objection.

When we speak of "contacts," we do not mean only face-to-face meetings; we also consider telephone conversations and mailed or faxed communications as contacts. In general, we find an average of between nine and 10 such contacts in a six-month period. This figure, interestingly, applies

Table 6.1

Client Satisfaction and Who Originates Contacts

Highly satisfied clients

Number of client-oriented contacts	1.7
Number of investment-manager-initiated contacts	7.8
Total contacts in average six-month period	9.5

Less-satisfied clients

Number of client-oriented contacts	3.7
Number of investment-manager-initiated contacts	6.2
Total contacts in average six-month period	9.9

both to high-net-worth clients who are highly satisfied with their interpersonal relationships with their investment managers and to those who are less satisfied [Table 6.1]. The significant distinction comes, as we said before, when we look at who originates the contacts. For the highly satisfied group, the investment managers originated most of the contacts; managers still initiated the majority of contacts for the less-satisfied group, but client-originated contacts increased significantly.

Besides correlating the origin of the contact with satisfaction levels, we also thought it would be worthwhile to break down the contacts by type (i.e., personal visit, telephone call, and mail or fax) [Table 6.2]. We

Table 6.2

Types of Contact and Originator

Contact type	Originator	Period 1	Period 2	Period 3	Period 4
Personal visit	Client	0.2	0.2	0.2	0.3
	Manager	1.7	2.2	2.2	2.0
Telephone call	Client	2.9	2.2	2.5	2.9
	Manager	2.0	2.3	1.9	2.1
Mail or fax	Client	0.2	0.1	0.1	0.1
	Manager	2.5	2.9	2.7	2.7

recorded these contacts over the two-year period of our study and found that basically the patterns once set tended to repeat themselves. (It should also be remembered that these observations record a bull market cycle in the equities market in the U.S.)

As is evident from the chart on types of contact, telephone calls are the most frequent means by which managers and clients communicate. We thus selected this medium for a closer study in which we correlate the originator of calls with levels of client satisfaction.

Month after month, quarter after quarter, less-satisfied clients are called less often by their investment managers. Perhaps this happens because investment managers prefer not to call clients who, they know or sense, are less than delighted with their performance; perhaps the investment managers just are infrequent callers, and this leads to a sense of neglect among clients and thus lack of satisfaction. In any case, the cycle appears stable over time, with less-satisfied clients consistently getting less attention from their managers.

The flip side of this phenomenon is that clients who feel they have to call more often than usual tend to be the relatively more dissatisfied ones. Clients who are less satisfied place twice the number of calls to their investment managers as clients who are highly satisfied [Table 6.3].

From the chart we see that less-satisfied clients are calling their managers more frequently than their managers are calling them, while the reverse holds for highly satisfied clients. Who places the call affects the basic dynamic of the relationship; the fact that telephone calls tend to be the most spontaneous form of contact makes these results all the more significant. The picture that emerges is, on the one hand (for highly sat-

Table 6.3

Originator of Telephone Contact and Satisfaction Levels					
Satisfaction level	Originator	Period 1	Period 2	Period 3	Period 4
Highly satisfied	Client	1.6	1.3	1.5	1.7
Less satisfied	Client	3.7	3.1	3.1	3.3
Highly satisfied	Manager	2.3	2.5	2.4	2.5
Less satisfied	Manager	1.8	2.0	1.7	1.9

isfied investors), that of a manager assiduously cultivating his clients, and on the other hand (for less-satisfied investors), that of the client anxiously or naggingly seeking out an unforthcoming manager.

We have identified nine or 10 contacts in a six-month period as an industry average. To be most effective, however, managers should determine the amount of contact with which each individual high-net-worth client is most comfortable. Some managers apparently believe that four times a year—once each quarter—is perfectly adequate; the numbers we have assembled in this chapter should serve as a wake-up call to these managers. Clearly, high-net-worth clients do not prefer to work in this way with their managers.

Besides looking at number of contacts and how they are initiated, we also asked our sample of investors about another side of attentive behavior: small gestures that communicate caring, interest and respect [Table 6.4]. These include small remembrances of a personal nature, such as birthday cards, sending clippings of interest, providing tickets to favorite activities and even remembering how coffee or tea is taken or the interests and schools of clients' children.

Some managers regard paying attention to these matters as a burden. The clients "should," these managers feel, focus on the rate of return of their money. One investment manager we talked to said that while the institutional clients concentrated on investment issues, the affluent

Table 6.4

Tangible Caring and Interpersoanl Satisfaction		
	Less satisfied	Highly satisfied
Manager puts forth a great deal of effort to make client feel like a valued customer	42.6%	64.2%
Often sends or gives something of a personal nature (birthday card, holiday gift, etc.)	72.3%	82.3%
Shows in many ways that he/she appreciates client's business	53.8%	78.0%
Shows they are very concerned about making the client a satisfied customer	47.0%	61.6%

clients seemed (frustratingly) to be more interested in irrelevant small talk about family. But it was precisely the high-net-worth side of the business that the investment manager needed to build up, since it accounted for 80% of the profits with just 20% of the assets the firm managed. The lesson is that attentive behavior matters too much to disregard; even if at times they seem a distraction from the primary business of investment management.

What we've seen in this chapter is that clients want to feel that their investment managers are paying attention to them. This attention can take the form of a telephone call—in many cases, that is the simplest and best thing to do. Personalized mail and fax communications, as well as personal visits, are also important. Gestures such as birthday cards and other remembrances also can contribute to client satisfaction.

Investment managers should think in terms of initiating contact with each affluent client nine to 10 times within a six-month period. This works out to once every two-and-a-half to three weeks. Of course, this number is drawn from industry averages; clients will each have their individual preferences. Managers should do their best to learn what these preferences are and then strive to accommodate them. Over time, investment managers should establish a personal communications plan for each affluent client based on the client's individual needs.

Managers should also be on the watch for clients who start initiating communications. Generally speaking, these clients are not satisfied, and thus these client-initiated telephone calls or other contacts can be construed as a warning flag.

In the next chapter we'll examine the last of the four components we identified as responsible for high levels of satisfaction with the client-manager interpersonal relationship: Shared values.

7

SHARED VALUES

Affluent investors, like most people, like to deal with others who share the same core values. Trustworthiness and those elements of personality that can be summed up as good manners also matter a great deal to high-net-worth investors. These are the areas we explore in this chapter.

First, we will consider the aspects of personality that have to do with similarity. People have long debated this question: how similar to his/her high-net-worth clients does a financial services advisor have to be to make them feel comfortable? For example, is it important for the advisor to come from the same social class? To have gone to the same schools?

In these cases, our research has produced quite clear-cut answers. These aspects of similarity are not important. Less than 20% of the investors we surveyed said that their primary financial advisors had an educational or social-class background that was similar to theirs. And none of the affluent said that their advisors had a lifestyle similar to theirs. There was basically no difference between investors who were highly satisfied and those who were less satisfied with their relationships with their financial managers on these questions.

One aspect of similarity does, however, hold importance for the affluent and also distinguishes highly satisfied clients from those less satisfied. It is whether or not the investment manager has values and beliefs similar to those of the affluent client. More than four-fifths of the highly satisfied clients said this was true of their investment managers; with less-satisfied clients, the number who affirmed this was somewhat under three-fifths [Table 7.1]. What seems to be happening is that skilled relationship managers learn about the attitudes, values and beliefs of their clients and mirror those back to them, creating an aura of similarity and a zone of comfort for the affluent client.

Granting that clients value a similarity in core beliefs with their managers, what, practically speaking, can managers do about this fact? Perhaps the most important skill managers need to develop is that of "reflective counseling." This ties in with the skill of reflective listening, involving listening with extreme care to the other person and reflecting back what they are attempting to communicate. In this way, the person sending the communication feels important, heard and understood.

Reflective counseling goes beyond reflective listening in that it relates directly to the investment services being provided. Specifically, reflective counseling involves educating the client about investment issues. Thus not only does the high-net-worth client feel a sense of comfort with the money manager, but the client also becomes better informed about the investment process. At the same time, the manager helps align the expectations of the client with reality.

Investment managers need to listen for the values and attitudes held by affluent clients and then indicate through words and behavior that these values are shared. The essential thing is for a manager to be able to do this even when the way in which a client expresses these values differs from the way the manager would do so. One of the most effective avenues to achieving this communication of shared values is to employ the Nine Profiles model described in *Cultivating the Affluent*.

The Nine Profiles model offers a framework for understanding the

Table 7.1

Kinds of Similarity and Interpersonal Satisfaction		
	Less satisfied	Highly satisfied
Manager has values and beliefs very similar to client	56.8%	82.5%
Has a background (education and social class) very similar to client	10.5%	11.4%
Has a lifestyle that is identical to client	0.0%	0.0%

basic motivations affluent clients have for working, on a discretionary basis, with a money manager. This knowledge enables managers to comprehend more readily the needs and wants of high-net-worth investors, as well as more effectively position their services and products to the affluent. In effect, the Nine Profiles scheme helps investment managers to a quick start in the process of achieving a high-quality interpersonal relationship.

As we indicated above, affluent investors are not looking just for similarity in core values in their investment managers. They also appreciate a host of behavior and courtesies that can be summed up under the rubric of good manners [Table 7.2]. All, or virtually all, of the high-net-worth investors who were highly satisfied with their interpersonal relationships said their managers were significantly more sincere, friendly, polite, respectful, caring and dependable than other top professionals; the less-satisfied group of investors was considerably less likely to agree with these characterizations. It should be emphasized that these are learned behavior,

Table 7.2

Good Manners and Interpersonal Satisfaction		
	Less satisfied	Highly satisfied
Manager is unusually sincere compared to other top professionals	64.9%	100.0%
Is much friendlier than other top professionals	59.1%	100.0%
Is significantly more polite than other top professionals	64.8%	100.0%
Treats clients with more respect than other top professionals	48.2%	100.0%
Is much more caring than other top professionals	46.7%	100.0%
Is unusually dependable compared to other top professionals	62.2%	100.0%
Is more personable than other top professionals	46.6%	98.8%
Is exceptionally courteous in dealing with clients	25.2%	98.8%

Table 7.3

	Less satisfied	Highly satisfied
Manager can be absolutely trusted to keep any secret client discloses	63.0%	100.0%
Has an unusually high degree of integrity	52.5%	100.0%
Keeps client's dealings completely confidential	73.0%	100.0%
Can be absolutely relied on to keep his/her promises	59.5%	100.0%
Is a very principled person, compared with other top professionals	67.8%	100.0%
Is far more honest than other top professionals	67.4%	100.0%

Trustworthiness and Interpersonal Satisfaction

which makes it all the more important for investment managers to incorporate them into their normal way of acting.

The third aspect of personality we wanted to take up in this chapter is trustworthiness and confidentiality [Table 7.3]. Affluent clients attach great importance to these values. The investors in the highly satisfied group unanimously felt that their managers could be completely trusted, were scrupulously honest and discreet and had high principles. Clients in the less-satisfied group were inclined to hold these views—more than half responded positively to each query—but they were far from unanimous.

Clearly, clients' feelings about the trustworthiness of their investment managers have a significant impact on satisfaction levels. To start with, managers can show by their statements and behavior that they agree with clients on the importance of these matters. Never discussing the affairs of another client and showing obvious care in the handling of client documents will help to convince clients that their managers are worthy of trust. One manager we know of makes a considerable effort to educate high-net-worth clients regarding the mechanisms employed by the firm to ensure confidentiality. Client feedback—which took the form of a near-doubling in referral levels as well as positive verbal communications—has convinced the manager to incorporate this material into the firm's promotional materials.

Communicating shared values and trustworthiness and at the same time exhibiting consistent good manners: these are vital elements in the process of building the kind of interpersonal relationship that yields high levels of client satisfaction.

A LAST WORD TO PART ONE

By and large, money managers do a good job of making their affluent clients happy when it comes to the performance of their investment portfolios. We could ask, though, how much of this satisfaction is attributable to a rising stock market in the U.S.? What will happen if the markets tumble, as they presumably will do someday? Will the investment performance satisfaction ratings tumble as well? It is quite likely this will happen, unless the money manager has done a good job of managing expectations and generating high levels of interpersonal satisfaction.

Why don't all money managers take the steps necessary to make certain their affluent investors are highly satisfied with the interpersonal nature of their relationship? One might guess that it is because they don't know what those steps are. Or because the steps are too difficult, too complicated, to implement.

Based on our extensive experience working with investment managers all over the world, these are not the reasons managers often fail to take the actions that would produce high levels of interpersonal satisfaction and build their businesses.

Lack of knowledge is not the problem. The specific behavior that creates high levels of interpersonal satisfaction have been clearly spelled out. Within each category of the I-CLAS methodology, we identified a number of components. Within each component, we looked at and evaluated specific behavior. The findings prove this is behavior that money managers need to adopt.

We have been able to identify this behavior and

its power to help build a money management business because many investment managers do in fact conduct their business and their actions in the ways indicated, producing high levels of interpersonal satisfaction. So the behavior specified is not too complex or difficult to be humanly possible.

In working with money managers, we find that the overwhelming majority know instinctively, if not on a cognitive or conscious level, about many if not most of the behavior we have been discussing. But we observe that time and time again, these same managers fail to act in ways that create highly satisfied affluent clients.

To a large degree, then, the issue is that of acting consistently rather than knowing what to do. One manager we talked to said he didn't have the time to do all "the unimportant things" that would endear him to his clients. However, it is precisely these "unimportant things" that are so important to growing a business.

We suggest that if your aim is truly to build your business, it is wise to make the time and take the appropriate initiatives. Money managers must consistently enact the behavior that builds high-quality interpersonal relationships. If this seems a great deal of work, remind yourself that referrals are a product of interpersonal satisfaction more than they are a product of investment performance satisfaction.

The objective should be to make this behavior virtually reflexive. Only when it becomes automatic, will its tremendous power be fully realized.

Perhaps understanding how potent this behavior is in growing an investment management business will prompt those managers who have not made it fully a part of their business life to move ahead and do so.

PART II

GETTING REFERRALS FROM ADVISORS: INSURANCE AGENTS, ACCOUNTANTS AND ATTORNEYS

1

UNDERSTANDING ADVISOR PSYCHOLOGY

As we stressed earlier, the first lesson for growing your money management business for high-net-worth clients is to keep clients highly satisfied. High levels of satisfaction produce referrals and additional assets from established clients.

But this process takes time. Investment managers aiming to accelerate the growth of their businesses will consequently want to look at the next best source of business development: referrals from other advisors to high-net-worth individuals.

We will discuss three different kinds of advisors: insurance agents, accountants and attorneys. It is absolutely essential for investment managers to realize that these advisors are not like money managers—and that they are also not like each other. They think differently, are paid differently, have different professional skills and ethical parameters and they have an altogether different professional psychology. Investment managers need to understand these differences both for the sake of working effectively with these other advisors in the interest of the client and for the purpose of gaining referrals from these advisors.

It might help, to bring this fact home, to call to mind the accountants, attorneys and insurance agents you know. It will probably not take much reflection to remind yourself how different these individuals are from each other. The differences arise, of course, from a variety of factors. Different types of people are drawn to each profession, and then each profession socializes its members in its own way. The structure of each profession creates different beliefs, values and business goals in its members. None of this can be ignored when seeking to create referral networks among advisors.

Investment managers who do ignore these differences will pay a heavy price in terms of business success. For example, we know of one investment advisor who developed a marketing program targeting both accountants and attorneys. It was a disaster. The accountants thought it was geared too much to attorneys. The attorneys viewed it as applicable only to accountants. It was a compromise that left everyone unhappy.

The lesson here is simple: over the long term, new client referrals will go to the managers and firms that devise referral systems that fit the psychology and professional culture of the different types of advisor. After studying advisors to the affluent over many years, we have found four major ways in which the professional culture of accountants, attorneys and insurance agents differs:

- Socialization into the profession: Each of these professions requires different, and specialized, training, which in effect socializes the new professional into the field. This process includes an exposure to the fundamental norms and values of the profession—its professional culture.
- Nature of the service: The exact nature of the service being performed is different for attorneys, accountants and insurance agents. The nature of the service—especially its frequency, scale and complexity—has a major impact on the relationship between the service provider and the client.
- Size of the client base: The nature of the service dictates the size of each professional's client base and also affects the degree of influence the professional has over clients' decisions.
- Sales orientation: The first three factors have major implications for how the different types of advisor compare on degree of orientation toward sales versus service.

In the remainder of this chapter, we will explore the professional psychology of advisors more deeply by looking at each of these areas of difference in more detail. Then we will highlight some of the conclusions that can be drawn from these differences.

Socialization

Attorneys undergo the most selective and rigorous training of the three groups. Law schools have historically been relatively difficult to gain entrance to, and the state bar associations maintain independent standards for admission. Training for accountants is more variable, depending on whether the CPA designation is sought. Hurdles to enter the insurance profession are lower, but the demands of the profession are such that many leave after just a few years. Corporate training programs, professional societies and outside vendors, rather than universities, provide professional education for insurance agents.

The professions differ in social status, the difference reflecting the relative degree of difficulty in entering the profession, how hard it is to create a sustainable practice, and the perceived social value of the services offered by each profession. Attorneys generally enjoy relatively high professional esteem (although threats to this status are revealed by the many lawyer jokes in circulation). Accountants are valued for the tangible contributions they make to company and personal financial management. Of these groups, insurance agents have the lowest social status, even though those at the top of the profession command very high incomes.

This process of professional socialization, and the consequent degree of social status, give members of the profession their sense of self and definition as professionals. It largely determines the way they see themselves in relationship to their clients and creates their professional culture.

This professional culture finds expression in many ways. One way involves the degree of ethical concern aroused by the issue of referrals. Some advisors find referrals ethically problematic, and, as a result, resist making them; other advisors do not see ethical dilemmas in making a referral. We will examine this matter in detail later in this book.

Nature of the Service

The nature of the service being performed, especially its frequency, scale, perceived risk and complexity, dictates the relationship between the advisor and the high-net-worth client in important ways [Table 1.1].

Compared to other advisors, attorneys tend to see their clients relatively infrequently. In addition, contacts are, more often than not, initiated by clients. Accountants, by contrast, tend to interact with clients periodically or even continuously over long periods of time, depending on the nature of the accounting services being performed. Insurance agents interact extensively with their clients in the early stages of a relationship as they assess the insurance portfolio, but then interaction drops off significantly. Unless the client brings up a new concern, there is little contact until the agent gets back in touch to review the account relationship.

The scale of the work performed also varies. If individual client projects are large, then fewer clients can be accommodated by a given advisor. This can be the case with accountants (if a client has contracted for many services, as privately held business owners may) and among attorneys (if the cases are large). Even among insurance agents, high-net-worth clients result in larger cases (and fewer clients).

We can also make distinctions in terms of the typical complexity of the services provided. Of course, there is significant variability in complexity within each profession; certainly some insurance work can be more complex than some legal work. However, in general, legal work is of moder-

Table 1.1

Distinguishing Characteristics of Advisors' Services to Their High-Net-Worth Clients

Service aspect	Attorneys	Accountants	Insurance agents
Frequency	On demand, client-initiated, infrequent	Continuous	Intense at beginning; then agent-initiated, infrequent
Scale	Driven by the magnitude of the case	Driven by client decisions to do "in-house" vs. retaining outside assistance	Driven by scales
Complexity	Moderate to high, depending on case	Low to moderate	Low to moderate
Client risk exposure	High, depending on case	Moderate	Low

ate to high complexity, while accounting and insurance work is (relative to other professional services) of low to moderate complexity.

But it is important to recognize that complexity tends to increase when the services in question are being provided to the affluent. For instance, insurance agents working with high-net-worth clients often sell life insurance as a by-product of providing estate-planning services. Obviously, these insurance agents must be, or quickly become, very adept at providing complex estate-planning analyses.

Size of the Client Base

The kind of service also affects the size of the client base each professional manages. Of the three professions in question, insurance agents have the largest set of clients [Chart 1.2]. Accountants occupy the other end of the scale, since their tasks tend to be time-consuming and recurring, as discussed above. Attorneys fall in between, but closer to accountants.

The clear implication is that insurance agents offer greater market potential, thanks to their larger client bases. We have seen instances in which an investment manager with access to the client base of a single insurance agent obtains a volume of referrals equal to what might be

Chart 1.2

Size of the High-Net-Worth Client Base

Insurance agents   Attorneys   Accountants

Many clients..Few clients

Client Base

gained from several accountants and attorneys.

For example, we know of one money manager who, working with a single insurance agent, garnered 43 new affluent clients in one year, for a total of slightly more than $76 million in new assets. Moreover, this manager expects to repeat these results for at least three more years—that is how many high-net-worth clients this insurance agent has worked with.

But there is another aspect of client-base size that managers need to understand. Specifically, the sheer size of the client base may mean that the advisor spends less time with any one client, and this distance can mean the advisor has less influence over decisions made by clients. In other words, the clients of many insurance agents may rely less on the suggestions and recommendations of their insurance agents than they do on the recommendations of their attorneys and accountants.

Sales Orientation

The three factors we have just discussed have implications for how much the different groups are sales-oriented. Insurance agents are sales-oriented; a great portion of their time is devoted to prospecting for new clients. Once clients have had an evaluation of their insurance portfolio, there is often little more that needs to be done with an account for a while, and the agent needs new business. For the most part, insurance is relatively front-loaded, and so agents have found a sales orientation to be most appropriate for the buying behavior of their clients.

Attorneys and accountants tend to be oriented to service, as opposed to sales. With accountants, this reflects the fact that customers tend to contract for the same services repeatedly over time, thus putting an emphasis on servicing current customers rather than prospecting for new ones.

Attorneys do casework. This implies an ongoing relationship with periodic, but relatively infrequent, contacts, alternating with spurts of high involvement when the client approaches the attorney with a specific problem. When the case is resolved, the relationships reverts to its low-

Table 1.3

Sales and Service Orientations Compared

Sales orientaion	Service orientation
Focused on transactions with clients	Focused on retention of clients through the creation of relationships
Measure of success is margin on sales	Measure of success is value of client relationship and goodwill
Short-term oriented	Long-term oriented
Typical of insurance agents	Typical of accountants and attorneys

key level. Attorneys emphasize service to insure that clients return with their next problem.

This sales/service contrast can also be seen in terms of contrast between an orientation towards transactions versus an orientation toward relationships. Transaction-oriented service providers focus on satisfying needs in the current exchange. By contrast, relationship orientations focus on creating value and quality for the customer over the longer term [Table 1.3].

We have sought to make clear in this chapter that other professional advisors do not see themselves in relation to their affluent clients in the same way that investment managers do. Insurance agents, attorneys and accountants differ from each other and from money managers. These differences in professional psychology arise naturally out of the varying ways in which the professions are entered, the socialization process for each occupation and the different nature of the work performed. Understanding these points of difference, and leveraging them, is a key to obtaining referrals.

Investment managers are sales-oriented, like insurance agents. Investment managers are highly oriented to grow assets under management, which entails prospecting for new client investors.

Investment managers share with accountants and attorneys their emphasis on client retention as well.

The major implication we see here is that attorneys, accountants and insurance agents will seek different benefits from their relationships with the investment manager. Consequently, successful money management firms will need to structure different schedules of rewards (for providing referrals) for each group of advisors.

In the following chapters we will examine these differences in more detail and discuss just what rewards are appropriate and effective with each advisor segment.

2

ADVISOR REFERRAL PATTERNS

Insurance agents, accountants and attorneys do generally refer their high-net-worth clients to investment managers. In this chapter we will examine the specifics of the way they do this—how many referrals they typically make in a year, whether they refer clients to just one or to several investment management firms, what percentage of their recommendations are acted on by clients, and other such matters.

Our findings draw on surveys of close to eight hundred advisors. (Specifically, we polled 363 insurance agents, 231 attorneys and 187 accountants.)

We believe that the patterns we have uncovered are of the first importance to managers seeking to grow their businesses. In essence, creating a referral network is a form of marketing, of selling the virtues of your firm to the advisors in question. As in any kind of marketing, the key steps are to segment the market, to set priorities for one's efforts and then to concentrate those efforts on the segments with the greatest potential. None of these steps can be taken without first gaining an understanding of basic facts about the market. Our surveys should help provide this essential groundwork of understanding.

The principles involved in successfully segmenting a market and setting priorities are simple. The best market targets should be significant in size, accessible to the marketers, and predisposed to the offerings of the marketer.

Considering our three groups (or segments) of advisors, life insurance agents meet these criteria best. They are numerous, identifiable and accessible to money managers and predisposed to make referrals, assuming that managers make it in their interest to do so. Attorneys and accountants also have excellent potential; we will look at them next.

Insurance Agents: The Top Priority

Insurance agents are a vast and relatively untapped source of referrals for investment managers. There are a number of reasons that investment managers should target insurance agents first.

- Agents make referrals. Agents focus their referrals. Although they will recommend several managers overall, they often recommend only one manager to a specific client. Attorneys and accountants generally recommend more than one manager to their clients.
- Agent referrals stick. When insurance agents make referral recommendations to their clients, high-net-worth clients follow through.
- Agents tend not to be approached by investment managers. Though accountants and attorneys have nearly all been approached by every type of money manager, insurance agents, to date, have not had the pleasure.

For a money manager, the payoff for a successful relationship with an agent will be a steady stream of referrals. Right now two patterns are starting to emerge. One is that many insurance agents are already making referrals to investment managers. The second is that agents are spreading their referrals around. This creates an enormous opportunity for investment managers.

Most agents do not yet feel that their relationship with any one investment manager is sufficiently positive that they should direct all their referrals to him or her. Instead, agents spread their referrals around in search of a mutually rewarding relationship. We have found that for the right package of investment expertise, client hand-holding and compensation, agents are willing to send all their referrals to one or two managers.

Another reason managers should target insurance agents is that they make referrals quickly. Almost one-half (49.5%) of the agents surveyed said they make referrals in a year or less [Chart 2.1]. Agents prefer to wait until they have completed most of their work with a client before making a referral, so they generally avoid making referrals in the first six months of working with a client. But once they have done what they can, insurance agents are very interested in making appropriate referrals.

In some ways, insurance agents can be simple to deal with because they are comparatively less interested in reciprocal referrals from the investment manager. While attorneys and accountants often want reciprocal referrals, insurance agents look for direct compensation. For attorneys and accountants, direct compensation is often not a possibility. Specifically, we found that only 6.1% of insurance agents are interested in cross-referrals, compared with 47.2% of attorneys and 58.9% of accountants.

As we indicated above, insurance agents are more likely than attorneys and accountants to recommend only one manager. Some 82.0% of agents name only one investment manager to their affluent clients, compared with 67.8% of accountants and 16.6% of attorneys. (The perceived fiduciary responsibility of accountants and attorneys, along with the sense that giving a client a choice of several managers leaves the final decision with the client, account for the greater caution of members of these professions.) Thus targeting insurance agents makes sense for the obvious reason that being the sole manager recommended is preferable to being one of several.

Chart 2.1

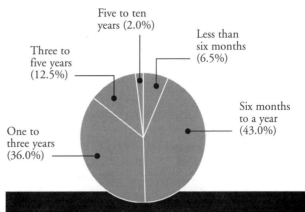

Five to ten years (2.0%)

Three to five years (12.5%)

Less than six months (6.5%)

One to three years (36.0%)

Six months to a year (43.0%)

Length of Client Relationship Before Referral is Made by Insurance Agents

And clients pay attention to the recommendations of insurance agents. Almost three-quarters of referrals (72.5%) from insurance agents are accepted by affluent investors. Accountants and attorneys also have high referral acceptance rates, 71.8% and 61.8%, respectively, but they are already targeted by a large number of investment managers.

The reason for the high acceptance rates is easy to understand. In these cases, high-net-worth customers have come to trust, value and depend on the professional skills of their advisor. By this point in the relationship, clients are in the habit of following the recommendations of their advisor.

Furthermore, insurance agents know how to sell. An insurance agent who makes more than 100 referrals (clients with minimum investable assets of $2 million) annually to investment managers explained that when he makes a referral, the affluent investor will always go along with the recommendation. The agent does all the selling, not only of the money manager but of the investment-management style employed by the money manager.

If you look at money managers seeking to cultivate advisors, you will find that they concentrate their efforts on accountants and attorneys. Thus accountants and attorneys are inundated with marketing materials, while insurance agents often do not appear on the radar screen of money managers.

Most investment managers have a bias against insurance agents. They picture someone badly dressed selling life insurance over a kitchen table. While it is fair to say that the greater number of insurance agents are not of interest to money managers, there are those who would make exceptional referral sources. These agents specialize in the upscale business owner and professional markets. They are involved in intricate and complex financial planning for their affluent clients. They are influential; their recommendations are well received. These are the insurance agents investment managers want to cultivate.

In time, these high-end insurance agents will be targeted as aggressively by investment managers as accountants and attorneys. At present, though, they are a largely untapped source of referrals.

But Don't Forget Accountants and Attorneys

We've indicated several reasons accountants and attorneys are less-rewarding targets for building a referral network than high-end insurance agents: they are generally slower in making referrals; they often already have a stable of preferred managers and they are more likely to offer a client a range of managers instead of just one. Notwithstanding these drawbacks, accountants and attorneys merit cultivation. The reasons are:

- Accountants and attorneys do make referrals.
- Being on a short list of recommendations is a lot better than nothing.
- High-net-worth clients take the recommendations of accountants and attorneys.

As we said above, accountants and attorneys are active referrers. More than 90%—93.0%, to be exact—of the accountants in our survey made a referral of a client to an investment manager within the past 12 months [Chart 2.2]. Attorneys are nearly as active—86.1% of our sample had made a referral in the past year.

We broke these numbers down by the number of referrals made to get a sense of what exactly is going on. We found that less than half of all accountants (44.3%) are very active in making referrals, referring 11 or more clients to investment managers in the past 12 months. About the same proportion (48.7%) referred between one and 10 clients to investment managers. Although accountants have a relatively small pool of clients, they can be fairly active in referrals thanks to the close relationships they enjoy with their clients. This closeness translates into trust and reliance on the part of their clients.

As we said, almost as many attorneys actively refer clients as do accountants, but not as many attorneys refer large numbers of clients. Specifically, about a quarter of the attorneys in our survey (25.1%)

referred 11 or more clients to investment managers in the past 12 months. A larger group (49.0%) referred between one and 10 clients in the same period.

We found that at present, accountants prefer to develop strong working relationships with a small number of quality investment managers. This situation makes it somewhat difficult for a new money manager to establish a new relationship with a referring accountant. Since accountants generally have experience in referring clients, they tend to have highly developed ideas about how the referral system has worked for them. Understanding the perspective of accountants on referrals will undoubtedly help managers in their efforts at market planning and obtaining a greater share of referrals.

It is important to remember that both accountants and attorneys are

Chart 2.2

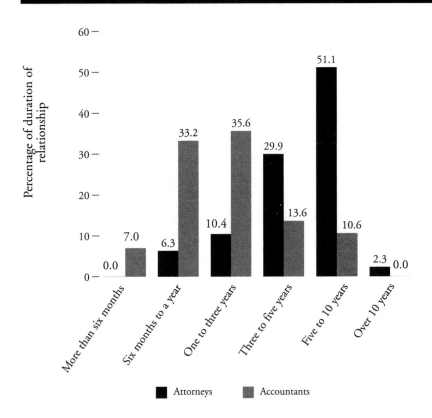

Duration of Relationship With The Client Before Referral is Made

Table 2.3

Concentration of Accountants' Referrals

Number of investment manager referrals made in the past year	Accountants making 1 to 10 referrals	Accountants making 11 or more referrals
One investment manager	40.7%	28.9%
Two investment managers	38.5%	50.6%
Three investment managers	14.3%	14.5%
Four or more investment managers	6.6%	6.6%

reluctant to make a referral before they have known the client for some time. This observation applies most strongly to accountants; they want to be very sure the relationship is well established before introducing new advisors into the mix. But, to a lesser degree, it also holds true of attorneys. The chart shows when, in the course of a client relationship, members of these professions refer a client to an investment manager.

We noted before that insurance agents spread their referrals around among a number of investment managers; this is not, in general, the case with accountants and attorneys. Members of these professions are more likely to concentrate their referrals among just a few managers. Thus the challenge is to get a spot on the "short list" of managers to whom attor-

Table 2.4

Concentration of Attorneys' Referrals

Number of investment manager referrals made in the past year	Attorneys making 1 to 10 referrals	Attorneys making 11 or more referrals
One investment manager	22.0%	74.1%
Two investment managers	24.8%	15.5%
Three investment managers	29.1%	5.2%
Four or more investment managers	24.1%	5.2%

neys and accountants feel comfortable referring their high-net-worth clients. There's no reason this cannot be done.

We'll look at accountants first. Most, as we said, make their referrals of high-net-worth clients to just one or two firms. With accountants who make 10 or fewer referrals, it breaks down fairly evenly between those who use just one firm and those who use two [Table 2.3]. Accountants who make 11 or more referrals are considerably more likely to use two firms.

When we expand our time frame to the past five years, we see quite naturally that both accountants and attorneys have interacted with larger numbers of investment managers. Time increases the range of contacts, and then over the years a winnowing process takes place. We looked at both the number of investment management firms with which accountants and attorneys have had professional dealings, and the number to whom they have made referrals. For both attorneys and accountants, we broke down our results by high- and low-volume referrers.

With accountants we find that over the greater time period, they have dealt with and referred to significantly more money managers than they do at present. This is especially true of accountants making one to 10 referrals; more than 97% of this group made referrals to four or more investment managers.

With attorneys the expanded time frame increases the number of money managers dealt with and referred to, but not as much as it does with accountants. About 60% of low-volume-referring attorneys have dealt with four or more investment managers, and about 46% of these

Table 2.5

Dealings of Accountants With Investment Managers Over The Past Five Years		
Number of investment managers accountants have dealt with in the past five years	Accountants making 1 to 10 referrals	Accountants making 11 or more referrals
One investment manager	0.0%	4.8%
Two to three investment managers	24.2%	38.6%
Four to five investment managers	12.1%	16.9%
Six to seven investment managers	14.3%	15.7%
Eight to nine investment managers	36.3%	22.9%
Ten or more investment managers	13.2%	1.2%

Table 2.6

Referral Patterns of Accountants Over The Past Five Years		

Number of investment manager referrals made in the past five years	Accountants making 1 to 10 referrals	Accountants making 11 or more referrals
One investment manager	1.1%	22.9%
Two to three investment managers	1.1%	10.8%
Four to five investment managers	30.8%	21.7%
Six to seven investment managers	28.6%	18.1%
Eight to nine investment managers	33.0%	25.3%
Ten or more investment managers	5.5%	1.2%

attorneys have actually made referrals to four or more firms [Table 2.4].

In a later section we will discuss the reasons attorneys and accountants drop some investment management firms after trying them out. In brief, we found that dissatisfaction with the relationship prevailed among the attorneys who switched, while with accountants the turnover probably

Table 2.7

Dealings of Attorneys With Investment Managers Over The Past Five Years		

Number of investment manager referrals made in the past five years	Attorneys making 1 to 10 referrals	Attorneys making 11 or more referrals
One investment manager	1.4%	12.1%
Two to three investment managers	38.3%	43.1%
Four to five investment managers	15.6%	24.1%
Six to seven investment managers	17.0%	15.5%
Eight to nine investment managers	27.7%	5.2%

Table 2.8

**Referral Patterns of Attorneys
Over The Past Five Years**

Number of investment managers attorneys have made referrals to in the past five years	Attorneys making 1 to 10 referrals	Attorneys making 11 or more referrals
One investment manager	15.6%	25.9%
Two to three investment managers	38.3%	50.0%
Four to five investment managers	19.9%	20.7%
Six to seven investment managers	22.7%	3.4%
Eight to nine investment managers	3.5%	0.0%

arose less from dissatisfaction than from problems with communication and trust. Over time, members of both professions focus their referrals on those investment managers with whom they have worked out mutually advantageous relationships [Tables 2.5, 2.6, 2.7, 2.8].

We also looked at a number of related issues having to do primarily with the readiness of high-net-worth clients to accept these advisors's referrals. Before we explore this, however, we should remind ourselves of how comfortable accountants and attorneys are with recommending just one firm.

As Table 2.9 shows, accountants are fairly ready to name just one firm,

Table 2.9

**Recommendation Patterns
of Accountants and Attorneys**

	Accountants	Attorneys
Recommended a single investment manager	67.8%	16.6%
Recommended more than one investment manager	32.2%	83.4%

Table 2.10

Accountants' Percentage of Referrals To Firm Most Recently Referred	
Less than 25%	55.7%
25% to 49%	20.7%
50% to 74%	6.9%
75% to 99%	2.3%
100%	14.4%

attorneys much less so. (In both professions, high-volume referrers—11 or more a year—are more likely to name just one firm; 75.9% of high-volume-referring accountants and 39.7% of high-volume-referring lawyers name just one money manager.) The reluctance of attorneys to give just one name arises from a heightened sensitivity to conflict-of-interest problems and concern over the possibility of litigation from a referral that doesn't work out.

We asked accountants what proportion of their total referrals are made

Table 2.11

Attorneys' Percentage of Referrals To Firm Most Recently Referred	
Less than 25%	3.0%
25% to 49%	25.6%
50% to 74%	28.6%
75% to 99%	24.2%
100%	18.6%

Table 2.12

Client Consideration of Other Firms

	Accountants	Attorneys
Other investment managers were considered	62.1%	50.8%
Other investment managers were not considered	27.0%	26.1%
Advisor does not know	23.1%	23.1%

(We'll observe parenthetically that a fairly large percentage—41.0%—of accountants who made a large number of referrals said their clients did not consider other investment managers.)

to the investment manager to whom they made the most recent referral [Table 2.10]. More than half—55.7%—said less than 25%; this pattern is mirrored by accountants referring different numbers of clients annually (64.8% of those referring from 1 to 10; 45.8% of those referring 11 of more). By contrast, only 14.4% sent all (100.0%) of their clients to this one investment manager.

Accountants tend to disperse their referrals; attorneys are less prone to do so [Table 2.11]. Consequently, a different picture emerges when this same question is asked of attorneys—more than 70% say they give half or more of their referrals to the firm to which they most recently gave a referral. Since attorneys usually give their clients two or more choices, it's

Table 2.13

Did The Client Ask Others About Recommended Investment Managers?

	Accountants	Attorneys
Other people were asked	79.9%	46.2%
Other people were not asked	6.9%	2.0%
Advisor does not know	13.2%	51.8%

more likely that a firm would have been named before.

Not surprisingly, most high-net-worth clients consider other firms as well, and not just those to whom they are referred or with whom they ultimately end up. Both accountants and attorneys affirmed this fact of life; accountants somewhat more emphatically. Table 2.12 gives the exact responses of both accountants and attorneys to the query of whether other firms were considered.

Clients also check out recommendations with trusted third parties [Table 2.13]. In cases where the advisor knows whether or not this was done, it appears overwhelmingly to be the practice. This points up the importance of word-of-mouth in the referral practice. It is imperative for investment management firms to establish and maintain strong reputations, because they do not control much of the information about their firm that is circulating in the marketplace.

In discussing insurance agents earlier, we emphasized that their referrals are accepted by a large percentage of clients. We'll finish this section by observing that the same observation can be made about the referrals of accountants and attorneys. Most clients do accept their referrals [Table 2.14]. Clients attach importance to the referrals of trusted advisors because investment management services are credence services, meaning they are sufficiently difficult and specialized that a layperson cannot evaluate them well. In the case of such services, people tend to rely heavily on the testimonials and recommendations of others; in this situation, their accountant or attorney.

What have we established? Briefly, it is as follows:

All types of advisors routinely make referrals of their high-net-worth clients to money managers. The practice of advisor referrals is well established. You do not have to change the natural behavior of advisors; you

Table 2.14

Referral Outcomes		
	Accountants	Attorneys
The client accepted the referral	71.8%	61.8%
The client did not accept the referral	28.2%	29.8%
Advisor does not know	0.0%	8.4%

just need to get into the referral flow.

Start with insurance agents. They make the best target market segment because they like to refer clients to managers, and they are willing to do so after a shorter (compared to attorneys and accountants) relationship with the client. They usually mention only one investment manager to the client, the client usually takes the recommendation, and (most important) they are a relatively untapped source of referrals for investment managers.

Absolutely, do not ignore attorneys and accountants, however. Attorneys and accountants are also active in making referrals, but slower to do so, and more careful about real or apparent conflicts of interest, as shown in their practice of including several managers in the list they provide to clients when making a referral. Don't push them to refer clients until they feel ready and don't try to make them refer only to you.

3

KNOWING WHICH ADVISORS TO TARGET

There are a great many insurance agents, accountants and attorneys out there. Which ones should you go after?

That's our topic in this chapter. Here, as elsewhere, we base our conclusions on data gained by communicating with the relevant professionals. This is really the only way to gain solid answers. Speculation might suggest that well-established professionals are the most rewarding target. After all, they have the largest client bases. But as it turns out, this approach is not optimal in the case of insurance agents, who should be, after all, the No. 1 target.

Our research indicates that your greatest efforts should be focused on insurance agents in the early stage of their practice, and accountants and attorneys at the peak of their professional years. Now we'll look at the findings that lead us to these conclusions.

Insurance Agents

There are more than 300,000 insurance agents in the country. If you market investment management services in a metropolitan or affluent suburban area, there are hundreds, if not thousands, of insurance agents. This creates a challenge for the money manager seeking to create referral networks—which insurance agents to target?

There are two main types of insurance agent: property, casualty and liability agents and life and health insurance agents. Property, casualty and liability agents who are well placed will have quite a few affluent clients among their customers, but they are not a particularly fruitful source of referrals. This is because these agents work intensively with an affluent client in the beginning to assess their property risks, but later contacts are limited to policy and coverage updates. They do not generally enjoy close, personal relationships with their high-net-worth clients because of the transactional nature of these relationships.

Life insurance agents, on the other hand, have more intense relationships with their high-net-worth clients. In the course of working up retirement, estate or business succession plans, they become quite knowledgeable about the client, the family, the family's business and the personal and business assets, including investments. They earn a position of trust and enjoy the confidence of their affluent clients. As a result, they are likely to know if their clients are seeking new money managers. Thus they make better prospects for a manager's referral network than do property and liability agents.

In particular, life insurance agents in the practice-building stages of their career cycle are good prospects. They empathize with investment managers who are at a similar stage in their careers and are more responsive to marketing overtures. Simply put, younger agents are hungrier.

As a result, managers seeking to establish referral relationships will have the best luck with insurance agents who make $100,000-140,000, annually [Table 3.1]. Most of the agents in these income categories (72.1% for the $100,000-120,000 bracket and 86.3% for the $120,000-140,000 bracket) actively make referrals of their high-net-worth clients to investment managers. Agents in other income tiers do not refer as actively.

Table 3.1

Income as a Referral Factor for Insurance Agents

Income of agent	% making referrals	% not making referrals
Less than $100K	0.0%	100.0%
$100K to $120K	72.1%	27.9%
$120K to $140K	86.3%	13.7%
$140K to $200K	36.3%	63.7%
More than $200K	43.5%	56.5%

Table 3.2

Age and Referral Activity Among Insurance Agents

Age	Referring agents	Nonreferring agents
25 to 34	32.5%	4.9%
35 to 44	53.0%	14.2%
45 and older	14.5%	80.9%

Age also correlates with referral activity [Table 3.2]. Most agents who actively refer clients to investment managers are in the 25-44 age range (accounting for 85.5% of referring agents). Agents 45 and older accounted for only 14.5% of referring agents. Older agents have existing client relationships and are less interested in pursuing referral business with money managers.

Data collected on educational background and years in the insurance business bolster these results [Tables 3.3 to 3.6]. More education goes with higher levels of referral activity, and younger people are, in general, better educated than are people of the previous generation. Agents with lower educational backgrounds and more years in the business are less likely to be active in referral relationships. They are also likely to be older

Table 3.3

Years in the Profession and Referral Activity Among Insurance Agents

Years in the insurance profession	Referring agents	Nonreferring agents
Less than 5 years	1.0%	2.5%
5 to 10 years	53.0%	24.5%
10 to 20 years	40.5%	25.2%
20 years or more	5.5%	47.8%

Table 3.4

Stage in Business Life Cycle and Referral Activity Among Insurance Agents

Stage in business life cycle	Referring agents	Nonreferring agents
Building	12.5%	4.9%
Growth	83.5%	53.3%
Established	4.0%	39.3%
Winding down	0.0%	2.5%

and to have higher incomes.

Taking all this information together, it is important for investment managers to recognize that there is a sharp generational divide between referring and nonreferring insurance agents. Older insurance agents operate the mature stage of their agency life cycle, spend relatively less time prospecting and are satisfied with the current scale and size of their agency or brokerage. In sharp contrast, agents who have created active referral networks with money managers tend to be younger, spend more time prospecting and are in the growing stage of their agency life cycle

Table 3.5

Prospecting Intensity and Referral Activity Among Insurance Agents

Percent of time prospecting	Referring agents	Nonreferring agents
40 to 54 percent	0.0%	4.9%
55 to 69 percent	10.5%	41.4%
70 to 84 percent	26.0%	27.2%
85 percent or more	63.5%	26.5%

Table 3.6

Education and Referral Activity Among Insurance Agents

Education	Referring agents	Nonreferring agents
Some college or less	9.0%	50.3%
College	75.0%	22.1%
CPA	6.0%	12.9%
Graduate or professional	10.0%	14.7%

[Tables 3.4 and 3.5]. (In our analysis of the business life cycle, we employ the classic four-stage model, involving a building stage, a growth stage, an "established" period and a winding-down stage.)

Gender does not seem to be a factor in referral activity [Table 3.7]. Women are a minority among insurance agents, but they are not disproportionately represented among either referring or nonreferring agents.

We have assembled the data supporting these observations in a number of tables. The tables correlate referral activity with the demographic factors we've discussed as well as such matters as stage in business life cycle and intensity of prospecting activity by the agent. Overall, these findings offer a fairly clear profile of referring agents.

Investment managers can tap into the younger successful agents in one

Table 3.7

Gender and Referral Activity Among Insurance Agents

Gender	Referring agents	Nonreferring agents
Male	82.0%	86.5%
Female	18.0%	13.5%

of three ways:

- Targeting wholesalers who sell insurers different products;
- Targeting producer groups and insurance brokerage networks—bands of successful agents who make deals with insurance companies to sell products at special rates; and
- Targeting individual agents.

Wholesalers can be located by reading the insurance literature as they are heavy advertisers. They can also be located by asking agents and by networking. Producers groups and insurance brokerage networks, which anecdotal evidence suggests are largely untapped, can also be found through networking. Individual agents can also be easily reached through networking.

Money managers should stress compensation and support services (such as training of agents and joint marketing efforts) when going after wholesalers, producers groups and individual agents. Seminars should include interactive training and custom-tailored concepts.

Some mistakes seem almost too obvious to mention, yet insurance agents say managers make them all too often. In any case, it's vital to avoid:

- A condescending attitude;
- Questioning insurance products the client has purchased; and
- Focusing on the manager rather than what is in it for the insurance agent.

Clearly, investment managers wanting to cultivate high-net-worth client referrals from insurance agents should do nothing to compromise the relationships insurance agents have with their affluent clients. Acting in such a way can only undo any sort of referral relationship.

We should mention one caveat regarding insurance agents. There is a trend in the insurance industry to move toward providing investment services. At an increasing pace, insurance agents are seeking to position themselves as asset gatherers, if not investment managers.

Insurance agents are selling more investment products than ever before. Variable products and mutual funds are a mainstay with many of them. We also see a growing interest in wrap products and fee-based discretionary accounts. Hence, insurance agents, while excellent allies in the near term, may become adversaries in the long term—competitors for the investable assets of high-net-worth individuals.

Accountants

The accountants to target are those with high incomes who are growing their businesses. These are the accountants who have already established themselves professionally, who have a well-established client base and who are ready to harvest the efforts of their younger years. Psychographically, they are more aggressive and growth-oriented than

Table 3.8

Age and Referrals Among Accountants

Age of accountant	Referring agents	Nonreferring agents
25 to 34 years	17.1%	15.4%
35 to 44 years	36.4%	38.4%
45 to 54 years	36.7%	30.8%
55 to 64 years	9.8%	15.4%

other accountants. Unfortunately, they are not easily distinguishable by age or years in the profession, although they will tend to be mature.

We've assembled some demographic and other information to help you in designing a marketing program aimed at this group of successful professionals. First, a word about gender. As a group, women make up less than 15% of accountants serving high-net-worth clients. Women generally have spent fewer years in senior positions in the accounting profession. In our survey, women made up 13.8% of the referring accountants and none of the nonreferring ones.

Other factors we explored had to do with age, income, stage of career development, growth in practice and related issues. We will look at these in turn. It should be clear that we are aiming to define a picture of your target market: accountants who refer.

Age is not a strong discriminator between referring and nonreferring accountants [Table 3.8]. Accountants who make referrals are concentrated in the 35- to 54-year age range (73.1%) in our sample. The same is true of accountants making no referrals (69.2% are in the same age range).

In general, referring accountants have higher personal incomes: 38.4% of those making referrals report personal incomes of $140,000 or more, compared to 0.0% of those making no referrals [Table 3.9]. Investment managers should target their market development effort toward these more successful accountants.

The rate at which income is growing correlates even more strongly with referral activity [Table 3.10]. There is a decided tendency for accountants who make referrals to report greater increases to their personal incomes: 90.3% say that their incomes increased 5% or more as compared to 38.4% of those making no referrals.

On the other hand, we found no significant difference between refer-

Table 3.9

Income and Referrals Among Accountants

Age of accountant	Accountants making no referrals	Accountants making referrals
Less than $100K	7.7%	2.8%
$100K to $120K	76.9%	42.0%
$120K to $140K	15.4%	16.8%
$140K to $160K	0.0%	23.0%
$160K to $180K	0.0%	9.9%
$180K to $200K	0.0%	3.4%
More than $200K	0.0%	2.1%

ring and nonreferring accountants with regard to the number of years spent in the profession or the stage of the business life cycle they had reached. For both groups, most of our survey sample had spent between 10 and 30 years in the profession. About four-fifths of each group (referring and nonreferring) said they were in the stage of growing their prac-

Table 3.10

Income Change and Referrals Among Accountants

Change in income of accountant	Accountants making no referrals	Accountants making referrals
Increase less than 5%	46.2%	9.7%
Increase 5% to 10%	23.1%	64.0%
Increase 10% to 15%	7.7%	17.3%
Increase 15% to 20%	0.0%	7.8%
Increase 20% or more	7.6%	1.2%
Decrease or no growth	15.4%	0.0%

Table 3.11

Growth in Practice and Referrals Among Accountants		
Change in accountants' practice size	Accountants making no referrals	Accountants making referrals
Increase less than 5%	46.2%	6.8%
Increase 5% to 10%	53.8%	54.3%
Increase 10% to 15%	0.0%	13.3%
Increase 15% to 20%	0.0%	11.6%
Increase 20% or more	0.0%	13.4%
Decrease or no growth	0.0%	0.6%

tice, with the remainder in the "established" period.

Accountants making referrals in general reported higher rates of growth in their practice—slightly more than half said their practices were growing by 5% to 10%, and most of the rest were seeing higher growth [Table 3.11]. (This goes along with the reported higher rates of income growth.) Investment managers sensitive to this orientation can identify accountants interested in growth and, consequently, also interested in referrals as a mechanism in that growth process.

Table 3.12

Prospecting Orientation and Referrals Among Accountants		
Percent of time spent prospecting	Accountants making no referrals	Accountants making referrals
Less than 10%	7.7%	8.9%
10% to 25%	69.2%	47.5%
25% to 40%	23.1%	27.3%
40% to 55%	0.0%	16.3%

Accountants spend much less time prospecting than do insurance agents [Table 3.12]. They prefer to devote most of their time to account maintenance. This is characteristic of their profession, as we saw when we explored professional cultures.

Still, an orientation to prospecting does tie in with referral activity. The only accountants who say they prospect as much as 40% to 55% of the time or more are those who are more aggressive about growing their practices and incomes (the same group that is active in making referrals). Accountants making no referrals report low levels of prospecting activity (74.9% say they spend less than 25% of their time prospecting).

The nature of the profession and the professional culture dictates that most accountants spend the bulk of their time in account maintenance; 98.8% of those referring their high-net-worth clients to investment managers spend more than 55% of their time in account maintenance. Virtually the same percentage holds for those who do not make referrals.

Most accountants referring high-net-worth clients feel their practices are not growing as rapidly as they would like [Chart 3.13]. This interest in growth ties in with the relatively high levels of interest in prospecting among this group and its emphasis on growing practice size and current income. It also explains much of the receptiveness to making referrals that is typical of the accounting profession, as will be discussed in a later chapter, and the interest in programs for client development. Because so many accountants want the future income streams created by increasing business, this desire becomes a significant leverage point for investment managers seeking to develop more extensive referral networks.

Chart 3.13

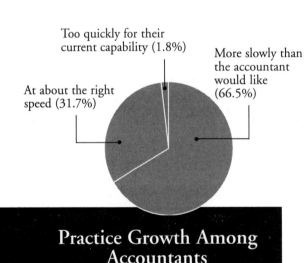

Too quickly for their current capability (1.8%)

More slowly than the accountant would like (66.5%)

At about the right speed (31.7%)

Practice Growth Among Accountants

Attorneys

Our survey of attorneys produced a less sharply defined picture of a referring attorney than what we obtained when we looked at accountants. Still, we observed a num-

Table 3.14

Gender and Referrals Among Attorneys

Gender of Attorney	Attorneys making no referrals	Attorneys making referrals
Male	87.5%	80.4%
Female	12.5%	19.6%

ber of significant distinctions.

Women (who make up just under 20% of our attorney survey group) are a little more likely to be found among the ranks of referring attorneys than among nonreferrers [Table 3.14]. And when we look at age, we see that the referring attorneys as a group are younger [Table 3.15].

Attorneys making referrals tend to have the higher personal incomes (66.0% report personal incomes of $160,000 or more, as compared to 43.7% of those making no referrals). Because the group of attorneys making no referrals includes those at the very beginning of their careers, that group also includes a significant proportion (34.4%) who earn under $120,000 at the low end for this group of attorneys [Table 3.16].

There is a slight tendency for attorneys who make no referrals to report greater increases to their personal incomes (43.8% say that their incomes increased 10% or more) [Table 3.17]. This may be attributed to steep

Table 3.15

Age and Referrals Among Attorneys

Age of attorney	Attorneys making no referrals	Attorneys making referrals
25 to 34 years	0.0%	3.0%
35 to 44 years	37.5%	48.9%
45 to 54 years	37.5%	48.1%
55 to 64 years	15.6%	0.0%
Over 64 years	9.4%	0.0%

Table 3.16

	Income and Referrals Among Attorneys	
Age of attorney	Attorneys making no referrals	Attorneys making referrals
Less than $100K	6.3%	0.0%
$100K to $120K	28.1%	6.5%
$120K to $140K	6.3%	14.8%
$140K to $160K	15.6%	12.7%
$160K to $180K	25.0%	43.5%
$180K to $200K	0.0%	16.8%
More than $200K	18.7%	5.7%

increases among those making the transition from associate to partner, or to increases in partnership share for new client generation. It should also be noted that the group of attorneys making no referrals also included a considerable fraction (25.0%) whose incomes were flat or went down.

The number of years in the profession does not have a major impact on

Table 3.17

	Change in Income and Referrals Among Attorneys	
Change in income if attorney's	Attorneys making no referrals	Attorneys making referrals
Increase less than 5%	3.1%	29.2%
Increase 5% to 10%	28.1%	51.5%
Increase 10% to 15%	40.7%	15.8%
Increase 15% to 20%	3.1%	2.8%
Increase 20% or more	0.0%	0.0%
Decrease or no growth	25.0%	0.7%

Table 3.18

Years in the profession	Attorneys making no referrals	Attorneys making referrals
Years in the Profession and Referrals Among Attorneys		
5 to 10 years	15.6%	0.0%
10 to 20 years	56.3%	51.0%
20 to 30 years	21.8%	39.0%
30 to 40 years	6.3%	10.0%
More than 40 years	0.0%	0.0%

referral activity, although we do see a concentration of junior attorneys in the nonreferring group [Table 3.18]. Specifically, 15.6% of those making no referrals say they have been in the legal profession less than 10 years.

We also asked our sample what stage of their business life cycle they had reached [Table 3.19]. The primary difference between the referring group and the nonreferring one here is that nearly one-fifth of the nonreferring attorneys said they were in the winding-down stage; none of the referring lawyers described themselves in this way.

In general, the differences in practice growth figures agree with what we would expect from the practice life cycle observations [Table 3.20].

Table 3.19

Stage in business life cycle of the attorney	Attorneys making no referrals	Attorneys making referrals
Business Life Cycle and Referrals Among Attorneys		
Building	0.0%	2.4%
Growing	53.1%	52.6%
Established	28.1%	45.0%
Winding down	18.8%	0.0%

Table 3.20

Change in Practice Size and Referrals Among Attorneys

Change in attorney's practice size	Attorneys making no referrals	Attorneys making referrals
Increase less than 5%	9.4%	13.0%
Increase 5% to 10%	59.4%	52.1%
Increase 10% to 15%	12.5%	11.2%
Increase 15% to 20%	0.0%	11.4%
Increase 20% or more	6.3%	8.4%
Decrease or no growth	12.4%	3.9%

The largest proportion who report no or declining revenues are those who also report they are winding down their practices (the attorneys making no referrals). Attorneys making referrals are somewhat more likely to report gains in practice revenues, but the differences are not marked.

Table 3.21

Prospecting and Referrals Among Attorneys

Percent of time spent prospectng	Attorneys making no referrals	Attorneys making referrals
Under 10%	0.0%	10.4%
10% to25%	21.7%	42.2%
25% to 40%	43.8%	26.3%
40% to 55%	9.4%	9.6%
55% to 70%	6.3%	8.4%
70% to 85%	6.3%	3.1%
85% or more	12.5%	0.0%

The nature and culture of the legal profession militates against spending large amounts of time prospecting for clients [Table 3.21]. The majority of both referring and nonreferring attorneys said they spent 40% or less of their time prospecting; in general, the referring group devoted less time to prospecting.

The other side of the coin to prospecting is account maintenance [Table 3.22]. In our study, 91.7% of those referring their high-net-worth clients to investment managers spend more than 55% of their time in account maintenance. Attorneys who make no referrals spend somewhat less time on account maintenance. This may reflect the senior, business development responsibilities of some members of this group.

As with accountants, most attorneys (72.1%) would like to see their practice expand at a faster rate. (One-quarter—25.4%—are content with the current rate of growth, while 2.5% say their practice is growing faster than their current resources allow for.) This interest in growth explains much of the receptivity to making referrals that is typical of the legal profession, and the interest in programs for client development and cross-referrals.

Most attorneys (86.1%) referred at least one client to an investment manager within the past year. Because attorneys are closely involved with estate and tax planning for their private clients, they are in a particularly good position to become aware of client dissatisfaction with a money manager. Because of their position of trust and confidence, their recommendations carry weight. Clearly, attorneys are worth cultivating; we've

Table 3.22

Account Maintenance and Referrals Among Attorneys

Percent of time spent on account maintenance	Attorneys making no referrals	Attorneys making referrals
Less than 10%	18.7%	0.0%
10% to 25%	0.0%	0.0%
25% to 40%	31.3%	0.0%
40% to 55%	37.5%	8.3%
55% to 70%	12.5%	54.7%
70% to 85%	0.0%	34.7%
85% or more	0.0%	2.3%

sought, in this section, to point out some salient characteristics of those who do make referrals.

Learning as much as you can about the target market is vital to any marketing effort. The results set forth in this chapter should help in that learning effort.

For accountants and attorneys, our advice here is similar. Go after growth-oriented professionals who already make referrals. Those making referrals constitute the majority in both professions, they're familiar with the purposes of referrals and some of the benefits, and they want to grow their practices. Accountants and attorneys who do not make referrals generally cite considerations of ethics and impartiality. It's hard to change such attitudes.

In targeting insurance agents, your emphasis should be on agents who are younger and actively seeking to grow their business. Also, go after life and health agents, as opposed to property and casualty agents.

Historically, investment managers have overlooked insurance agents as a source of high-net-worth client referrals. Therefore they represent a key opportunity for money managers who are alert and energetic.

4

KEY TO GETTING REFERRALS

Various strategies are available to investment managers seeking to motivate advisors to provide referrals. One is compensation, either on a fixed-fee basis or as a percentage of assets. Another is cross, or reciprocal, referrals. Still another is joint marketing program support. This chapter examines which strategy to use with each kind of advisor.

Compensation for Referrals

The old saying "money makes the world go around" has application in this business as well. Compensation for referrals is a potent strategy. It is, however, appropriate only for one advisor segment—life insurance agents. In general, accountants and attorneys do not feel they can legitimately accept direct monetary compensation for referrals to investment managers.

Insurance agents, on the other hand, are fairly direct and unapologetic about receiving monetary compensation from money managers for referrals. In most cases, insurance agents expect to receive compensation for making the referral, and the more clients they refer, the more they expect to be paid. We found that more than three-quarters of the insurance agents who make referrals said they expected and in fact received compensation for the referral. (By way of contrast, no attorneys or accountants who made referrals admitted to expecting or receiving monetary compensation.) In fact, our experience leads us to believe that even the numbers we report here are underestimated because of the sensitivity of this issue. Compensation affects the frequency of referrals and it affects who gets the referrals.

Monetary compensation is thus the key to capturing referral business from insurance agents, who constitute potentially the most productive target market for investment managers. Money managers should move now to establish relationships with insurance agents as they are a relatively untapped source of business, and many are still unaware they can be compensated for providing referrals. Moreover, by moving quickly, investment managers are creating allies instead of potential competitors.

Our survey covered 200 insurance agents who made referrals. Some 77.0% of these, or 154 agents, said they expected to receive compensation and did receive it (the other 23%—46 agents—did not expect compensation, and may or may not have actually received it). Seven of those 154 also obtained compensation from clients. Almost 45% of the 154 agents did not inform clients they expected to receive compensation from money managers. Just over 55% said they did inform clients.

Money managers now have the upper hand in these relationships, but whoever has the affluent clients controls the game. Insurance agents will soon become much more knowledgeable. On the one hand, investment managers are slowly seeking to cultivate insurance agents as a referral source. At the same time, insurance agents are moving into the investment management business. The advantage will go to those investment managers who move expeditiously to create an environment that is financially beneficial to the insurance agent.

Right now, agents are compensated in a number of different ways and compensation rates vary widely. For example, insurance agents report compensation agreements ranging from highs of 25 basis points annually on assets of $1 million or more to lows of 5 basis points annually.

Some agents report a finder's fee arrangement: the insurance agent makes the referral and is paid a flat or graduated fee for a set period of time. The best arrangement of this kind has the insurance agent receiving 100% of first-year investment management fees, 50% of the second year's investment management fee, 10% of the third year's and 5% in year four and after. This arrangement is comfortable to many insurance agents as it mirrors their compensation arrangement when they sell life insurance.

The variety in compensation arrangements often makes agents uncomfortable. Insurance agents do not know what standards to apply, and they do not know what to expect from money managers.

We asked agents about compensation arrangements and got a range of answers [Chart 4.1]. There is still sensitivity about the issue, so these numbers are low. More than 20% of the agents compensated by man-

Chart 4.1

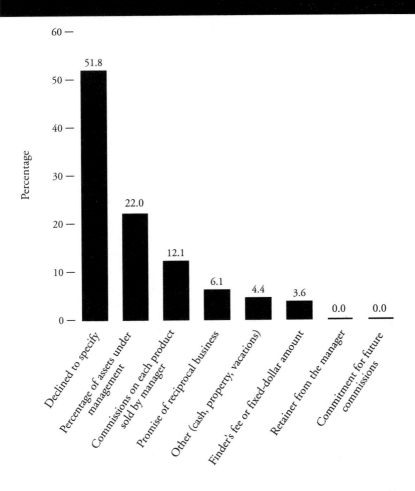

Type of Compensation to Agents for Most Recent Referrals

Percentage

- 60
- 51.8
- 50
- 40
- 30
- 22.0
- 20
- 12.1
- 10
- 6.1
- 4.4
- 3.6
- 0.0
- 0.0
- 0

Declined to specify

Percentage of assets under management

Commissions on each product sold by manager

Promise of reciprocal business

Other (cash, property, vacations)

Finder's fee or fixed-dollar amount

Retainer from the manager

Commitment for future commissions

agers said they received a percentage of the clients assets under management for their most recent referral. About 12% said they received a commission for each investment product sold to a client they had referred. But half declined to specify the type of compensation received. Such information is often confidential, and agents may make separate arrangements with different managers.

Although compensation is a potent key to obtaining referrals from insurance agents, managers should not assume agents know of these

Table 4.2

Reasons That Some Agents Do Not Make Referrals	
You have not been approached by money managers offering training and education in exchange (either implicitly or explicitly) for referrals.	87.0%
You have not been approached by money managers offering reciprocal referrals.	62.0%
You have not been approached by money managers offering compensation for referrals.	60.5%
You were not aware you could be compensated for referrals.	59.5%
You prefer to direct your clients to the money management products you sell.	43.6%
You do not find any benefits in referring business to money managers in exchange for commissions.	37.4%
You want to remain impartial, so you do not provide referrals.	0.0%
You feel it's unethical to provide referrals for money managers in exchange for commissions.	0.0%
You may have a fear of litigation in the event the money manager performs poorly.	0.0%

opportunities. In fact, many do not. Close to 60% of 163 insurance agents who did not actively refer said they were unaware they could receive compensation from money managers or had not been approached by managers offering compensation or reciprocal referrals.

Based on industry trends, we think compensation agreements will become standardized over the next three to five years. Money managers should establish relationships with insurance agents now before agents become committed to other relationships. Managers should expect to raise compensation and to expand relationships to include such value-added components as joint-marketing efforts to retain relationships.

In general, the reason for insurance agents not making referrals is that they have not been approached [Table 4.2]. Agents who haven't made a referral in the past 12 months say they have not been approached with a offer of training (87.0%), with an offer of reciprocal referrals (62.0%) or an offer of compensation (60.5%). More than half were unaware they could receive compensation for referrals (59.5%).

Clearly, a significant opportunity exists for money managers to develop new channels of distribution through intermediaries in the insurance industry. Almost half of the agents in our survey are not in the habit of referring; many because they are unaware of the benefits.

Although some do not refer for competitive reasons—they offer similar investment vehicles—this group is smaller than those who are simply ignorant of the incentive programs money managers have created to make referrals worthwhile to insurance agents. As previously noted, the trend in the insurance industry is to provide investment services. Sophistication concerning investment management services among insurance agents is very likely to rise as the industry moves in this direction.

All (100%) of the agents and brokers who sell their own money management services are aware that money managers will generally pay compensation of some sort for referrals. Similarly, all of those who were not aware money managers paid compensation for successful referrals do not sell their own money management services.

The incentives that appeal most to insurance agents share the characteristic of being immediate in benefit. Direct payments linked to the value of the referral are broadly popular. These payments could be commissions on the basis of each product sold by the money manager or compensation based on a percentage of the referred client's assets (both favored by more than 95%). Another alternative agents would not object to would be a finder's fee or some agreed-to fixed-dollar amount for each referral (favored by 100% of nonreferring agents who did not know about compensation arrangements). Insurance agents who offer their own money management products are still interested in referral programs with a strong cash compensation or prospecting program component. It may be that they see that it would be more efficient to refer such clients to specialists if the reward structure were sufficiently attractive.

Agents are also open to help in prospecting. It should be recalled that almost all of these agents, even those with established agencies, spend most of their time prospecting for new affluent clients. Selling an affluent prospect or managing the relationship with an affluent client is not perceived as nearly as arduous a job as prospecting. However, the effect of these prospecting programs must be short term and positive, or interest in making additional referrals will drop off significantly.

Measures such as noncash-incentive programs (e.g., vacations), general education programs, networking opportunities among other advisors and promises of some future compensation generally hold little appeal for insurance agents.

There are a few differences in reactions to incentive programs based on the reasons agents do not make referrals now. Agents who currently sell money management products are much more interested in an ongoing retainer arrangement from the money managers they refer to than are other agents who are not doing any current referring. This group (those who currently sell investment products) is also much less interested in incentives such as reciprocal business or in educational opportunities showing them how to sell more of their services to their current clients. Table 4.3 shows the level of interest in a range of incentives for each group of nonreferring agents.

Table 4.3

Percent of Nonreferring Agents Voicing Interest in Various Incentives		
Type of incentive	Nonreferring agents who sell money management products	Nonreferring agents who were unaware of compensation for referrals
Commission on each product sold by money managers	98.6%	96.7%
Joint prospecting programs (joint seminars, joint advertising, etc.)	97.2%	90.2%
Compensation based on a percentage of the client's assets given to the money manager	95.8%	98.9%
Information on how to prospect, sell and work with the affluent	87.3%	80.4%
Finder's fee or fixed-dollar-amount compensation per referral	81.7%	100.0%
Retainer from the money manager	71.8%	39.1%
Reciprocal business	28.2%	90.2%
The money manager showing how its services will enable you to sell more of your services to your clients.	21.1%	92.4%
Other types of payments (cash, property, vacations, etc.) from the money manager	9.9%	4.3%
Education on the products the money manager sells	2.8%	5.4%
Education on changing social and tax situations that affect your client.	2.8%	32.6%
Commitment for future commissions from the money manager	0.0%	2.2%
The money manager creates the opportunities for you to network with other types of advisors to the affluent	0.0%	0.0%

Reciprocal Referrals and Marketing Support Programs

If direct compensation is out—as in general it is—the question aris-es: What should you do to get referrals from accountants and attorneys? The answer is simple: offer cross-referrals and other marketing support opportunities.

The Big Six accounting firms are registered investment advisors, and a number of law firms have asset management arms. These professionals are looking for new ways to keep their core businesses strong and refer-rals of new clients are the key. To capture referrals successfully, managers must provide specific details at face-to-face meetings on how they can help these accountants and attorneys with cross-referrals and other mar-keting support.

Most accountants and attorneys say they already get cross-referrals from investment managers. More than half of accountants (59.9%) and almost as many attorneys (47.2%) expect cross-referrals as a result of their referrals to managers, and other data shows that accountants and attor-neys do receive referrals from investment managers. All the attorneys and accountants we polled said they did not expect commissions, finder's fees, retainers or other forms of direct compensation.

In thinking about this subject, it's important to keep in mind the interests of accountants and attorneys. Members of these professions focus on long-term, mutually rewarding relationships with their affluent clients. They think in terms of client lifetime value. Their main concern is to keep their clients satisfied with their relationships. If they can assist in finding managers who will also satisfy their client's service and perfor-mance expectations, so much the better. This way of thinking explains why so many accountants insist that they want their clients to work with high-quality investment managers (95.4%). For attorneys, the number is only slightly lower—84.4%.

For both attorneys and accountants, the referral begins with the high-net-worth client. Typically, the client becomes dissatisfied with the cur-rent investment manager and asks the advisor for a referral to a new money manager. Client dissatisfaction was cited as the trigger by 86.2% of accountants and by 78.9% of attorneys.

Both professions attached considerable importance to the investment manager providing reciprocal referrals, and the feeling that the invest-ment manager in question was well-suited to the particular high-net-worth client. A significant change in the client's circumstances was an important factor in making a referral for more than two-fifths of the accountants we surveyed and for a quarter of the attorneys. Roughly one-third of the attorneys considered it important that the investment man-ager provided business-building educational programs or worked with the attorney to grow his/her business; these kinds of effort mattered less

Table 4.4

Importance of Various Factors in Making a Referral

	Accountants	Attorneys
You want to make sure your client works with a high-quality investment manager.	95.4%	84.4%
Client dissatisfaction with his/her current investment manager	86.2%	78.9%
Significant change in the client's circumstances	44.3%	25.8%
The investment manager provides reciprocal referrals.	37.9%	54.5%
You thought the specific investment manager would be more appropriate.	32.8%	64.1%
Client required specialized investment advice.	15.5%	16.1%
The investment manager provides educational programs that helps to build your business.	14.9%	37.2%
The investment manager periodically works with you to build your business.	11.0%	32.2%
The investment manager provides networking opportunities from his clients.	4.0%	2.5%
You receive compensation for making the referral from the investment manager.	0.0%	0.0%
You receive compensation for making the referral from the client.	0.0%	0.0%

to accountants.

In Table 4.4 we show the exact percentage of attorneys and accountants who considered these and other factors important in making a referral. It is perhaps worth pointing out again that no attorney or accountant cited direct compensation as a factor.

We also investigated the factors that control the choice of a specific investment management firm for accountants and attorneys. For both professions, the firm's track record with clients previously referred to it ranks as most important. This makes sense, since both professions are focused on their long-term relationships with their clients; jeopardizing a client relationship by making a referral that offers some short-term benefit is not in the interest of either attorneys or accountants.

Still, members of both professions showed high levels of interest in cross-referrals from investment managers [Table 4.5]. Recommendations from professional colleagues and the image of the firm also mattered to both lawyers and accountants. Attorneys were sensitive to the consideration that the firm be of sufficient quality to make litigation unlikely, while

Table 4.5

Importance of Various Factors in Selecting a Particular Investment Manager

	Accountants	Attorneys
Track records with previous clients	79.9%	72.9%
Recommendations from professional colleagues	67.2%	52.8%
Expectations of referrals from the investment manager	59.0%	53.3%
Image of the firm	53.5%	49.2%
Local pressure	33.9%	10.1%
Recommendations from previous clients	16.1%	10.1%
Loyalty to the investment manager	8.0%	14.1%
Marketing education program provided by the investment manager	6.3%	10.1%
Reduction of the risk of client litigation	5.2%	43.7%
Technical education program provided by the investment manager	5.2%	34.2%
Length of the relationship	1.1%	3.5%
Personal relationship outside work	0.6%	0.0%
Recommendations from social acquaintances	0.6%	0.0%
Type of compensation (fixed-fee or percentage)	0.0%	0.0%
Amount of compensation offered by the investment manager	0.0%	0.0%
Type of compensation pay schedule (short- or long-term)	0.0%	0.0%

a significant minority of accountants valued a firm with a local presence.

In planning reciprocal referral programs, investment managers should be careful that they can honor their commitments. Most attorneys and accountants receive referrals from a small circle of investment managers —three or fewer, usually, and of course the same ones to whom they send their referrals. And the number of referrals accountants and attorneys receive is small—typically it is one to three over a five-year period.

Most accountants and attorneys in our survey do make a practice of referring their high-net-worth clients to investment management firms (generally, when asked to do so by their clients). A minority of each pro-

Table 4.6

Reasons Nonreferring Accountants and Attorneys Do Not Make Referrals

	Accountants	Attorneys
You feels it's unethical to provide referrals to investment managers in exchange for commission.	92.3%	96.9%
You want to remain impartial, so you do not provide referrals.	84.6%	13.4%
You have a fear of litigation in the event the investment manager performs poorly.	30.8%	56.3%
You have not been approached by investment managers offering training and education in exchange (either implicitly or explicitly) for referrals.	7.7%	0.0%
Providing referrals is outside your area of expertise.	0.0%	25.0%
You have not been approached by investment managers offering reciprocal referrals.	0.0%	0.0%
You were not aware you could be compensated for referrals.	0.0%	0.0%
You prefer to direct your clients to the money management products you sell.	0.0%	0.0%
You do not find any benefits in referring business to money managers.	0.0%	0.0%

fession, however, does not. Why is this?

The answer is clearly not what it was for many nonreferring insurance agents—that they hadn't been approached by investment management firms or were unaware of the benefits arising from referrals. In general, the nonreferring accountants and attorneys were fully aware that money managers wanted their clients and would seek to make it worth their while to refer them. Attorneys and accountants who did not make referrals overwhelmingly said they considered it unethical to refer clients to investment managers in exchange for compensation. A large majority of nonreferring accountants also cited the desire to remain impartial as a reason for eschewing the practice, while the fear of litigation figured prominently among attorneys. Table 4.6 gives the precise percentages of accountants and attorneys who cited these and other factors as important in the decision not to make referrals.

It's worth remembering that the number of accountants and attorneys who do not make referrals is fairly small. In general, it is not realistic for investment managers to think they will have much success in changing such fixed, and principled, ideas.

For insurance agents the optimal scenario is direct monetary compensation based on referrals made. Joint-prospecting approaches will also enhance the motivation of insurance agents to work with money managers.

Money managers must get the message out that they want to work with insurance agents. There are numerous ways this can be accomplished, including:

- Attending insurance industry conferences;
- Public relations programs that communicate your desire to work with insurance agents who focus on upscale markets;
- Direct marketing efforts and
- Developing relationships with producer groups and insurance brokerage networks.

Insurance agents represent an exceptional opportunity for investment management firms. It's critical, however, to recognize that these insurance agents can also become competitors. One way around this possible conundrum is to empower agents to market your investment services directly.

One insurance brokerage network we know of focuses on the investment management and trust services of a private bank with which it had established a relationship. The insurance agents in the network market the mutual funds, discretionary investment management services, and trust services of the private bank. The agents are compensated with an ongoing fee for their efforts; they also get technical and marketing support from the bank. While the fees are essential, the latter services keep this insurance brokerage network loyal to the private bank.

As we have seen, most attorneys and accountants make referrals in the expectation of cross-referrals. Members of both professions tend to wait until an affluent client relationship is cemented before making a referral to an investment manager. (This is particularly true of accountants.) When they make a referral, they will provide the names of several investment management firms. (Attorneys do this more than accountants.) They say they do not expect compensation and that they have not received any.

Many accountants and attorneys already refer clients, so managers interested in getting a share of these referrals should concentrate on convincing them that they are better suited to service clients than the managers these advisors currently recommend. Managers can do so by offering details of their track record and examples of how they solved specific servicing needs.

For accountants, personal testimonials and personal experience weigh heavily in the referral process. Investment managers should therefore emphasize networking approaches in developing this market. Specifically, they should:

- Offer seminar and conference presentations to build awareness of and respect for their services;
- Obtain testimonials from satisfied clients and other accountants to use in developing new professional referral relationships;
- Make clear their intention to cross-refer clients for accounting services and
- Avoid emphasizing direct compensation for referrals.

In approaching law firms, investment managers should emphasize opportunities for joint client development through seminar selling, and also demonstrate that a sufficient volume of cross-referrals can be maintained. As with accountants, it does not pay to focus on direct compensation for referrals.

Accountants and attorneys who do not now refer clients to investment managers are small minorities of each profession, and resistant to changing views on what they regard as issues of principle. Since this is the case, it makes sense to concentrate on attorneys and accountants who are already comfortable with the referral process. Communicate a concern for ethics to these professionals; it may happen that some nonreferring accountants and attorneys will come to participate through the means of joint prospecting seminars and such efforts.

How, specifically, can you make contact with accountants and attorneys? Attend local and national CPA and bar association conferences and seminars, or organize your own. Given their need for continuing education about tax and legal issues, these intermediaries are highly receptive to such forums.

In the next chapter, we'll look at techniques for positioning your business to make it more attractive to advisors.

5

THE ART OF SUCCESSFUL POSITIONING

Thoughtful investment managers will recognize that compensation and marketing support programs are not, in and of themselves, sufficient to create and sustain a rewarding network of referring advisors. For all advisors—accountants, insurance agents and attorneys—client relationships are too hard-won to risk losing them because of a poor referral.

Over the years, advisors will generate far more revenues through their direct relationship with a high-net-worth client than they ever will through a referral. So, for an advisor to achieve the greatest benefit from a client relationship, they have to make good referrals to managers—the kind that result in highly satisfied affluent clients.

Thus, for managers, the challenge is to convince advisors you are the sort of money manager to whom it would be good to refer high-net-worth clients. The way to do this is to position yourself and your practice appropriately. Several steps are involved:

- Decide on your personal positioning
- Deal with advisors' perceptions
- Reinforce your positioning

We'll look at each of these steps in turn.

Your Personal Positioning

The first challenge for investment managers is to position themselves personally with advisors. Positioning is simply the art of creating the right impression. Indeed, positioning has been called impression management.

Most investment managers have this skill already.

Money managers position themselves with their high-net-worth clients all the time. They actively work to create a particular impression, one intended to draw new high-net-worth clients to the money manager as well as help to maintain those relationships.

Some managers position themselves as technical experts. Others position themselves as wise counselors and advisors. Still others play the role of innovators at the cutting edge of investment science. Money managers position themselves to play to their strengths and to help affluent clients know what to expect in working with them.

Positioning also works when managers seek to create relationships with advisors. Managers should have a strategy for how they want to be positioned with advisors; that is, how they want advisors to think of them. Is it as a good business partner? As a solid affluent client manager? As an attentive provider of feedback?

After determining how they want to be perceived, managers must in part overcome preconceived ideas that advisors may have. (We look at these ideas in the section below.) Then, investment managers need to communicate this image to their target advisors. The means of communication with each type of advisor have already been discussed. Obviously, if the message does not get out, the advisors will not be aware of you and your services.

Advisors' Perceptions

Investment managers do not position themselves in a vacuum. They work against a background of existing perceptions that advisors already have of money managers. To assist your efforts at positioning, we decided to examine these perceptions, looking specifically at how the different types of advisor regard various kinds of money manager.

It turns out that most advisors do not think highly of investment managers. Insurance agents tend to rate managers more positively than do other advisors, while accountants are the harshest critics and attorneys fall in the middle (but closer to accountants). Overall, though, existing perceptions of investment managers are not highly favorable. Why is this?

With insurance agents, it probably reflects the fact that money managers have not always managed their relationships with insurance agents very well. Also, it should be remembered that the perceptions are just that—perceptions, not realities. With attorneys and accountants, the lack of esteem may have something to do with the fact that members of these professions, because of their confidential relationships with their clients, hear many "horror" stories about the failings of money managers.

In any case, the negative perceptions, whatever their source, actually represent an opportunity. They mean there is plenty of room for a committed money manager to shine.

We looked at perceptions of a variety of kinds of money manager—independent investment managers, brokerage houses, private banks and so on. (It should be emphasized that we asked about impressions of each category of money manager, not about specific individuals or firms.) We measured the percentage of advisors who rated each type of manager as "extremely good." And we asked this question both about investment expertise and about service quality, or how the relationship (as opposed to the money) was handled. Some money managers fared well in one area, but not the other.

It might be thought that we employed a rather stiff test in looking just for "extremely good" ratings. But we have found this the best way to study the issue. "Extremely good" ratings correlate strongly with quality, satisfaction and long-term relationships. And how many advisors will refer clients to managers they view as "fairly good?"

Looking at insurance agents first, we see that perceptions of excellence in investment expertise often do not go along with perceptions of excellence in service [Table 5.1]. Multioffice independent investment managers were most likely to be deemed extremely good in investment expertise, but only 2% of agents thought they deserved that rating in service quality. Local independent money managers, on the other hand, obtained fairly high ratings in both areas. Local private banks and trust

Table 5.1

Percent of Insurance Agents Rating Money Managers as "Extremely Good" in Portfolio Management and Personal Rapport		
	Portfolio Management	Personal Rapport
Multioffice (multistate) independent investment managers	68.5%	2.0%
Local independent investment managers	67.0%	47.5%
Independent trust companies	56.5%	21.5%
National brokerage houses	56.0%	0.0%
Local brokerage houses	37.2%	0.0%
Multioffice (multistate) private banks and trust companies	0.0%	0.0%
Local private banks and trust companies	0.0%	43.5%

companies got better-than-average ratings in service, but abysmal ones in investment expertise. The chart gives the exact percentages for each category of money manager.

In general, insurance agents need reassurance from all managers about investment performance. Managers from private banks and trust companies should go out of their way to discuss their investment performance track record with doubtful agents in order to position themselves as successful investment firms, while managers from national or multistate operations need to work on their service image.

Accountants, as we indicated earlier, are not overawed by money managers [Table 5.2]. In assessing portfolio management, about a quarter rated multioffice, independent money managers as extremely good; a smaller number awarded this designation to local independent investment managers and national brokerage houses. (Apparently, specialization—this is what independent money managers offer—is seen as a plus by at least some accountants.) No other types of money manager got any "very good" ratings in portfolio management. On the service side—specifically, the ability to develop personal rapport with clients—only local private banks and trust companies and independent trust companies were seen worthy of "extremely good" ratings, and these only by fairly small minorities. Accountants who made many referrals did not differ

Table 5.2

Percent of Accountants Rating Money Managers as "Extremely Good" in Portfolio Management and Personal Rapport

	Portfolio management	Personal rapport
Multioffice (multistate) independent investment managers	24.1%	0.0%
Local independent investment managers	16.1%	0.0%
National brokerage houses	14.9%	0.0%
Local brokerage houses	0.0%	0.0%
Local private banks and trust companies	0.0%	21.3%
Independent trust companies	0.0%	9.2%
Multioffice (multistate) private banks and trust companies	0.0%	0.0%

Table 5.3

	Portfolio management	Personal rapport
Percent of Attorneys Rating Money Managers as "Extremely Good" in Portfolio Management and Personal Rapport		
Multioffice (multistate) independent investment managers	35.7%	38.7%
Local independent investment managers	30.2%	12.6%
National brokerage houses	25.6%	0.0%
Local brokerage houses	21.7%	0.0%
Local private banks and trust companies	0.0%	19.2%
Independent trust companies	0.0%	10.1%
Multioffice (multistate) private banks and trust companies	0.0%	0.0%

significantly from those who made just a few.

Attorneys also regard specialization as a plus in portfolio management, with independent money managers (both local and multioffice) winning the most "extremely good" ratings in this area [Table 5.3]. On the matter of personal rapport, attorneys favor locally oriented firms. Local independent investment managers and local private banks and trust companies got the most "extremely good" ratings. As with accountants, the number of referrals an attorney made did not affect the ratings.

We also sought to get a fix on advisors' perceptions by using a technique known as perceptual mapping. We asked advisors to rate the various kinds of manager on a scale of one to 10 (one being the worst and 10, best) in two different areas or dimensions: service quality and investment expertise. We then used the numbers to plot a grid; service providing one axis and investment expertise, the other [Chart 5.4]. This mapping offers a readily accessible way of seeing how the types of money manager compare with each other in the perceptions of advisors. It can help managers by showing the strengths they should emphasize in their marketing, as well as by identifying weaknesses where greater effort is required.

We'll see first what this method yields with regard to the perceptions of insurance agents. Overall, local independent money managers are

Chart 5.4

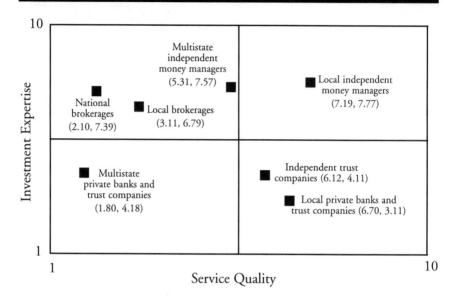

positioned best. Insurance agents think these providers do the best job in terms of both investment expertise and service quality. Insurance agents tend to feel that local managers maintain warm interpersonal relationships with clients. These money managers should emphasize their specialty in particular investments.

Multistate or national money managers also fare well; although insurance agents are less confident of their service quality, which comes in at 5.31 on the one-to-10 scale. These investment managers should emphasize their ability to provide service, explaining how the level of contact is governed by client needs and preferences and how the managers stay on top of the account.

Local private banks and trust companies and independent trust companies come up short in the area of investment expertise, with scores of 3.11 and 4.11, respectively. But they pull rankings of 6.70 and 6.12, respectively, when it comes to service. These providers should tell agents how they manage portfolios and underscore strong performance histories.

On the flip side, insurance agents see wirehouses as offering strong investment management but feel that they do not understand high-net-worth clients and offer poor service. Brokers must rectify this perception by

Chart 5.5

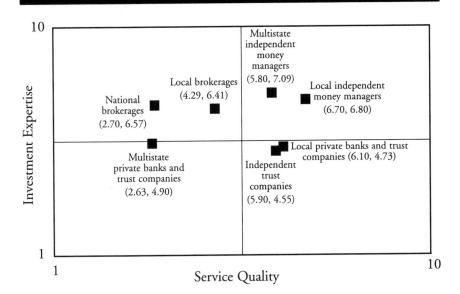

Perceptual Map: How Attorneys Rate Financial Services Providers

showing how they meet the ongoing service needs of clients. They need to get past the image of an impatient broker taking a short call from a client. Brokers should familiarize themselves with the range of consultancy services that brokerages offer today and the related client-servicing issues.

Multistate private banks and trust companies have the steepest hill to climb, scoring low in investment management (1.8) and below average (4.18) in service quality. These firms need to spend the most time with agents, showing how these firms can meet local client needs and offer an array of investments that local providers cannot always match.

We assembled perceptual maps for attorneys and accountants, as well [Chart 5.5 and 5.6]. The results show that these professionals are highly unsatisfied with the services of high-net-worth investment managers, giving them poor marks on both performance and service. Investment managers looking to get referrals should tout their strengths to attorneys and accountants but should not initiate discussions of their perceived weaknesses. This contrasts with the approach we advise for insurance agents, where managers should confront negative views head-on by showing how they perform better than competitors.

The difference springs from the fact that attorneys and accountants

Chart 5.6

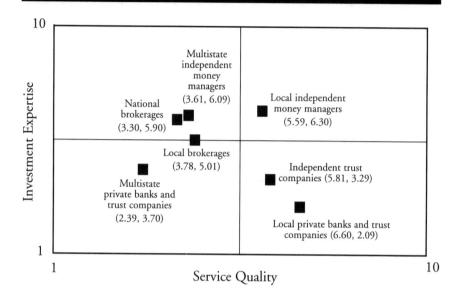

Perceptual Map: How Accountants Rate Financial Services Providers

10

Investment Expertise

Multistate independent money managers (3.61, 6.09)

National brokerages (3.30, 5.90)

Local independent money managers (5.59, 6.30)

Local brokerages (3.78, 5.01)

Multistate private banks and trust companies (2.39, 3.70)

Independent trust companies (5.81, 3.29)

Local private banks and trust companies (6.60, 2.09)

1

1   Service Quality   10

have even more negative views of money managers than do insurance agents. Consequently, managers would just reinforce shortcomings in the eyes of these intermediaries by bringing up negatives and would damage chances to get referrals from them. So don't invite the negative comments, but be ready to respond to them when they come.

Local and national independent money managers fare the best on the ratings by lawyers and accountants. But even these money managers rack up only middling scores on our one-to-10 scale.

In attorneys' eyes, national private banks and trust companies do a poor job in client relationships (2.63) and also deliver inferior portfolio management (4.90). These national firms must be ready to demonstrate that, even though they often offer a wider range of investments than local firms, they maintain strong client relationships in the community. Local institutions of all types tend to be rated higher by attorneys than their national counterparts. Letters of referral may be useful in persuading attorneys that money managers are good at maintaining long-term client relationships.

Accountants also regard positively the notion of local presence. In fact, large institutions are seeking to build regional identities by opening up local branches in many states, including Florida and California. If a provider today cannot build a local office or convince intermediaries of its commitment to local clients, then it should show in some other way what differentiates it from competitors.

Accountants rate local banks and trust companies the highest on the service dimension, but rate their investment performance close to the bottom (6.60 and 2.09, respectively). They are also not impressed with money managers and brokerages, rating their client service at 3.78 or lower.

Overall, most types of money manager are not well thought of by these advisors. This may be unpleasant news, but the process of correcting wrong or negative perceptions has to start with seeing exactly what those unwanted perceptions are.

Reinforcing Your Position

After establishing a relationship with advisors, investment managers should keep at work on the job of positioning themselves. They need to refine their approach based on the type of advisor being dealt with, as well as the strengths and weaknesses of their own firm.

With insurance agents, for example, investment managers should talk about their investment specialty, what makes them different from their competitors. Managers should also discuss compensation arrangements for the referral. More than 70% of the 200 insurance agents surveyed say it is very important that money managers contact them frequently to inform them about new incentives for referrals; making these frequent contacts is a way of reinforcing your position.

With attorneys and accountants other tactics may be useful, such as providing evidence of ability to develop close personal relationships with clients. We must also emphasize that advisors want peace of mind—as much as it lies within your power, you should make it clear that your actions will not jeopardize their relationship with the client.

The single most important fact established in this chapter is that the advisors we are talking about do not in general have especially favorable impressions of investment managers. And this means that a strategic opportunity lies open to investment managers who can deliver quality and at the same time convince advisors they are doing so—that is, position themselves effectively.

We have observed that accountants and attorneys generally agree that specialization is best, and that investment management firms that are specialized perform better for their clients. Regardless of their institutional status, investment managers would do well to emphasize their independence within whatever corporate structure they find themselves. They should, of course, be able to demonstrate that their performance is competitive across the range of investment managers.

Insurance agents also show a higher regard for independent investment management firms. It may be that insurance agents, who themselves run small businesses, identify with the entrepreneurial nature of such firms. In any case, it is a value to be kept in mind when dealing with this group of advisors. Most important, insurance agents are looking for investment management firms that can deliver for their affluent clients as well as for them.

6

HOW TO CEMENT RELATIONSHIPS WITH ADVISORS

Referrals from advisors can play a vital role in growing your high-net-worth money management business. But it must never be forgotten that each relationship with an advisor needs to be nurtured as carefully as a relationship with an affluent client. Each relationship takes effort, persistence and empathy. We've grouped the efforts you can make to cement your relationships with advisors under six headings. These are:

- Network
- Trust
- Satisfaction
- Communications
- Proactivity
- Relationships

In this concluding chapter, we look at each of these in turn.

Network

The first step in constructing a referral network that will sustain your investment management business for years to come is to develop individual relationships with advisors. We suggest you begin with the advisors you already know, and who know your work. You may be surprised at how many of these there are.

The next stage is to branch out to the advisor groups you have explicitly targeted. Unless there are compelling reasons to the contrary, we believe that the initial target should be younger insurance agents with strong, but growing, practices themselves.

There are several ways to meet advisors. One of the most effective is through referrals from your own high-net-worth clients. The odds are very good that each one of your affluent clients uses the services of an accountant, attorney and insurance agent.

Another effective way to meet advisors is through other advisors. Most advisors know of other professionals who provide services to high-net-worth individuals. There are also the many seminars and workshops that serve the respective industries.

Insurance agents tend to be most accessible at conferences and seminars, so that's where investment managers should seek high visibility. Managers can set up exhibition booths at conferences to offer material on their firms. Some attractive conferences include the Million Dollar Roundtable (members are agents who have sold at least $1 million of insurance a year) and the Association of Advanced Life Underwriters.

Investment managers can also target the study groups in which insurance agents share information about industry trends and sales practices. Managers can ask agents they already know how and when to attend such meetings. As we indicated earlier, for insurance agents the focus should be on bolstering areas of relative weakness rather than talking about acknowledged strengths.

For meeting accountants and attorneys, you should attend and, ideally, make presentations at the seminars and conferences these advisors often attend to continue their professional educations. As you become comfortable with the structure and value of these conferences, you could consider hosting your own and arranging for continuing education credit. It is worth noting that many states also require insurance agents to obtain continuing-education credits.

We know of a number of managers who have created successful referral networks through this approach. One investment management firm provides educational seminars explaining the basic principles behind investing. These workshops discuss the risk/return tradeoff and introduce the basic styles of investing, such as value versus growth. The firm does not push its own investment style nor does it even bother to discuss its services. Instead, the workshops are purely educational. Those advisors who are interested in learning more about the firm (approximately 40% per workshop) are met with individually. Of course, all attenders receive continuing-education credit.

One factor makes this networking approach particularly effective, and that is that insurance agents, accountants and attorneys are all seeking to create relationships with investment advisors. They are looking for you at the same time you are looking for them. We know this because of the importance of word-of-mouth.

Word-of-mouth is extremely important in building awareness and creating business alliances with advisors of high-net-worth clients. All advisors making a referral need to feel comfortable with the risks involved. Since your investment advisory services are complex and hard to evaluate directly, most advisors also rely on the testimonials of others in making their decisions about managers.

Our emphasis on word-of-mouth, seminars and conferences emerges directly from our research. We asked insurance agents, accountants and lawyers about the significance of various channels of information about investment managers. Each group ranked information from professional colleagues (word-of-mouth) top, followed by seminars and conferences held by investment managers. No other source of information was nearly as important. Table 6.1 lists the different channels of information we asked about, and what percentage of advisors (grouped by profession) deemed it important.

Table 6.1

Factors Important to Advisors in Learning About Investment Managers			
	Insurance Agents	Accountants	Attorneys
Information from professional colleagues	86.0%	51.1%	78.4%
Seminars and conferences held by the investment manager	61.0%	48.3%	39.9%
Third-party introduction to an investment manager	13.5%	5.8%	0.0%
Seminars and conferences held by third parties	7.5%	9.2%	0.0%
Recommendation from organizations or associations of which you are a member	6.5%	0.6%	0.5%
Cold call from an investment manager	6.5%	0.6%	1.0%
Information from other types of advisor	4.0%	2.9%	0.5%
Promotional materials from the investment manager	1.5%	4.6%	11.1%
Information from clients	0.0%	9.2%	1.0%

While the factors other than word-of-mouth and conferences are of secondary significance, they should not be totally discounted. Many advisors rated them as having "some importance." Speaking practically, receiving promotional materials from a investment manager will not put that firm on the short list of preferred partners for referrals, but if that investment manager is recommended by a trusted colleague and something is known about them because of promotional materials, then the recommendation is reinforced and a referral is more likely to occur.

How advisors network has something of a bad-news, good-news quality to it. The "bad news" is that they network among one another, and this information flow you can do relatively little about, directly. Indirectly, you can have an aggressive public relations campaign and be persistent in asking advisors to introduce you to other advisors, but at the end of the day, word-of-mouth is hard to control.

The "good news" is that advisors learn about investment managers almost as much through seminars and workshops. These you can control. You can organize them, and you can become active in industry conferences. The other good news is that advisors are seeking to find new, qualified and reliable investment managers almost as eagerly as you are seeking them.

Trust

Meeting advisors who can make referrals may or may not be easy, but a bigger task—perhaps the biggest—comes next: creating trust between you and that advisor. You are asking that advisor to entrust you with one of their most prized assets—a high-net-worth client. They will not make that referral until they feel they can trust you not to damage the relationship of trust and confidence they have with their client.

These are real concerns. The investment manager may perform unsatisfactorily, thereby eroding confidence and trust. The money manager may disagree with recommendations of the advisor and urge the client to take different actions, thus undermining the authority of the advisor.

Trust is even more crucial when future compensation for a current act is involved; as when advisors make referrals in the expectation of either compensation or reciprocal referrals. For example, when an insurance agent's compensation is based on some data over which they have no direct control (i.e., a percentage of assets or future earnings), agents need to be able to trust that investment managers are being fair. When accountants or attorneys refer in the expectation that reciprocal referrals will be forthcoming, trust in the relationship is equally critical. (We should mention that investment managers need, in particular, to understand the professional culture of the insurance industry, which is highly competitive, even cutthroat at times. Insurance agents are not predisposed to trust other professionals in client-service situations.)

Overall, we found that levels of trust between advisors and investment managers are relatively low. This represents a tremendous opportunity for managers to bridge this gap. We explored advisors' feelings in this area by asking a number of related questions: whether the advisor considered the money management firm trustworthy, whether the manager could be relied on to keep his/her commitments, whether the manager was a bit insincere, or not above "bending the facts," and so on. Table 6.2 gives the responses to these and other queries for each type of advisor. Some differences exist between insurance agents, attorneys and accountants, but the evident fact is that no

Table 6.2

Advisors Rate Trust in Investment Managers

	Insurance Agents	Accountants	Attorneys
The investment manager can be relied on to keep his/her commitments.	52.8%	50.8%	41.2%
You find it necessary to be cautious in dealing with the investment manager.	46.2%	42.4%	44.8%
There are times when you find the investment manager to be a bit insincere.	41.9%	19.7%	44.8%
The money management firm is trustworthy.	22.0%	51.8%	13.2%
The money management puts the client's interests above its own.	11.6%	12.6%	7.5%
The money management firm is not above "bending the facts" in order to sell more.	7.5%	6.5%	12.1%
The money management firm and you are in competition because you both provide some of the same products.	4.5%	0.0%	1.1%
You suspect the money management firm sometimes withholds crucial bits of information that might affect the client's decision.	2.5%	4.5%	6.9%

group displayed a great deal of trust in money managers. Advisors who felt higher levels of satisfaction with their investment managers were more likely to trust them. This is not surprising: satisfaction and trust go hand in hand.

Converting an advisor-acquaintance to an advisor-referral source involves creating trust. The general absence of trust between advisors and managers represents the single biggest opportunity available to investment managers. It is crucial for investment managers to understand, and empathize with, the risks advisors take in making referrals, and to overcome this feeling of risk and distrust. Doing this involves a number of specific actions and attitudes. We discuss these in the rest of this chapter, but in brief, the more important initiatives include:

- Openness about the referral process in any seminars and relationship-selling efforts investment managers undertake;
- Frank discussion of the compensation system or reciprocal referral program, and procedures for valuing each referral;
- Assurance of immediate feedback to referring agents on the outcome of the referral;
- Timely settlement of any compensation that is owed and
- Ongoing feedback about the client.

Satisfaction

As we explored in the first half of this book, and as most money managers know intuitively, satisfaction is a critical factor in any financial services relationship. It is the single most important thing managers can do to grow their own businesses. Simply put, the highly satisfied high-net-worth customer is more likely to:

- Place additional assets under management;
- Refer other high-net-worth individuals to the investment manager; and
- Brush off overtures by other investment managers.

On the other hand, the dissatisfied high-net-worth customers is likely to:

- Pull assets and
- Discourage other high-net-worth customers from using the investment manager.

Managers must recognize that it costs 10 times more in time and effort to get a new client than it does to ensure that a current client is satisfied. Smart (and efficient) managers focus their attention on current clients and strive to satisfy them knowing that in the long run, this is the most efficient way to build a successful practice. Highly satisfied clients will praise the investment manager to their advisors, reinforcing the tendency among advisors to refer other clients.

Having reiterated the importance of satisfying clients, it will probably be no surprise when we say that it is also essential to satisfy the advisors from whom you are seeking referrals. But when we look at this key business-building component, we find a situation similar to what we found with trust. A significant percentage of advisors is not especially satisfied in their dealings with investment managers.

We polled advisors on two issues—1) whether they would describe themselves as "very" or "extremely" satisfied with their investment managers, and 2) whether they thought the clients they had referred were "very" or "extremely" satisfied with the manager. About half of the insurance agents and attorneys said they were satisfied to this degree (a little more than half for insurance agents, a little less than half for attorneys). A little more than three-fifths of accountants said they were "very" or "extremely" satisfied. With regard to their beliefs about clients' satisfaction, the numbers were not greatly dissimilar: slightly less than half of insurance agents, more than half of attorneys, and three-quarters of accountants believed their clients were "very" or "extremely" satisfied with their investment managers [Table 6.3].

Perhaps we should emphasize that these numbers do not refer to feelings about money managers in general; these are considered assessments by advisors of how satisfied they have been with the particular relationships they have experienced. They tell us that large numbers of advisors are not particularly happy with these relationships. Obviously, this widespread dissatisfaction creates tremendous opportunities for managers who

Table 6.3

Advisor Satisfaction With Referrals	
	Very or extremely satisfied
Insurance agents	
Personal satisfaction with the investment manager	54.8%
Perception of clients' satisfaction	45.2%
Attorneys	
Personal satisfaction with the investment manager	47.7%
Perception of clients' satisfaction	56.3%
Accountants	
Personal satisfaction with the investment manager	62.6%
Perception of clients' satisfaction	75.3%

can deliver high levels of satisfaction. When others do poorly, it's easier to succeed. Without altering our basic message, we can add as a refinement that the volume of referral activity has a bearing on satisfaction. Attorneys referring more affluent clients are far more likely to be highly satisfied (77.6%) than are attorneys who refer fewer clients (35.5%). The same relationships hold true in attorney's perceptions of their clients' satisfaction; 82.8% of attorneys referring 11 or more clients say they believe that the clients are very satisfied. It is to be expected that attorneys who have more experience working with investment managers and referring clients to them would be more highly satisfied. On the other hand, the relatively low satisfaction of attorneys referring fewer clients creates an opportunity. Investment managers who can create a convincing demonstration on why attorneys would be more satisfied with referrals to them will be able to induce some attorneys to make a trial referral or two.

The number of referrals made also matters somewhat with accountants. Accountants referring more clients are more likely to say their clients are highly satisfied (81.9%) than are accountants who refer fewer clients (69.3%). Their evaluation of their own relationship does not vary with the number of clients referred in the past year. We do observe that very satisfied accountants are more likely to concentrate their referrals on just one or a small number of investment managers.

Since accountants are comparatively more satisfied with the outcomes of their referrals, investment managers will have to work somewhat harder to establish a new referral relationship with them. They will have to give accountants a compelling reason to change from their current referral patterns.

Overall, however, the absence of high levels of satisfaction among advisors stands as a great opportunity for energetic investment managers.

Communications

The ways in which managers communicate with advisors are of absolutely vital importance to the referral process. Indeed, we found that the mistake managers made most often is perhaps the easiest to avoid: they lose referrals because they fall into what we have termed the communications trap. By this, we mean that money managers often fail to communicate in the ways or on the subjects that advisors want; when managers do communicate, often it is on subjects not regarded as important by advisors. But these patterns can be changed, and doing so produces happy (and referring) advisors. It sounds simple because it is.

What kind of communications do advisors want? The answer varies with the type of advisor. Insurance agents are most interested in learning about new incentives for referrals. Accountants overwhelmingly want feedback on clients they have referred to the money manager. (Insurance agents and attorneys also rated feedback highly.) Attorneys want to hear about new training opportunities; they are also quite interested (as are accountants) in new products and services the manager might offer.

Table 6.4 shows the different kinds of communication we asked about, and what percentage of each type of advisor considered the communication important. It is striking that one kind of communication that money managers frequently make—inquiring if the advisor has any new referrals—won virtually no rankings as important by advisors.

We also looked at the frequency with which different kinds of communications are made, as perceived by advisors [Table 6.5]. This varied by type of advisor, but it is worth noting that in no case did a majority

Table 6.4

Percent of Advisors Who Say It is Important That The Investment Manager Contacts Them Frequently in Order to...

	Insurance Agents	Accountants	Attorneys
Explain new incentives for referrals	72.9%	5.7%	1.0%
Tell you how they handle referrals	62.3%	48.0%	9.1%
Provide feedback on other clients you have referred	52.8%	94.8%	54.3%
Tell you about new training opportunities they provide	16.0%	14.9%	63.1%
Announce new products and services they have available	15.0%	48.6%	34.2%
"Stay in touch" for other reasons	11.0%	29.3%	12.6%
Find out about changes in your practice and clients	6.5%	10.3%	29.1%
Do something of a personal nature (e.g., birthday card, holiday gift)	1.0%	0.6%	1.5%
See if you have any referrals to make	0.5%	0.0%	0.0%
Tell you about changes in laws and regulations that might affect your client	0.0%	0.0%	27.6%

of advisors say they were frequently contacted with a communication they considered important. (Fairly large minorities of accountants and attorneys did, however, say that managers frequently made communications of a kind they considered important.)

Investment managers, as we indicated above, fall into the communications trap when they fail to communicate frequently on the subjects advisors deem important. They commit a similar, perhaps less-grievous, sin when they communicate all too frequently on matters advisors regard as secondary. What we have in mind here is that some advisors resent the nagging persistence (as advisors see it) with which money managers call to ask if there are new referrals.

Table 6.5

Frequency of Communications From Investment Managers, as Perceived by Advisors

	Percentage agents say frequent	Percentage accountants say frequent	Percentage attorneys say frequent
See if you have any referrals to make	44.2%	48.9%	52.3%
Tell you how they handle referrals	22.5%	18.4%	1.5%
Find out about changes in your practice and clients	18.1%	4.0%	15.1%
Tell you about new training opportunities they provide	15.5%	12.1%	35.2%
Do something of a personal nature (e.g., birthday card, holiday gift)	14.0%	14.9%	9.5%
Provide feedback on other clients you have referred	13.0%	38.5%	19.7%
Announce new products and services they have available	5.0%	10.9%	26.1%
"Stay in touch" for other reasons	2.5%	5.8%	1.5%
Inform you of new incentives for referrals	1.0%	0.0%	0.0%
Tell you about changes in laws and regulations that might affect your clients	1.0%	0.0%	10.1%

These failings are widespread. Insurance agents, accountants and attorneys each have their own views on what they want to hear about

Table 6.6

Insurance Agents' Perceptions of the Communications Trap

Importance and frequency of communications	Important communications	Less-important communications
Received frequently	None	See if you have referrals to make
Received infrequently	Inform you of new incentives for referrals; Tell you how they handle referrals; Provide feedback on other clients you have referred	Tell you about new training opportunities; Announce new products and services; Stay in touch; Find out about changes in your practice; Do something personal; Tell you about changes in laws and regulations

Table 6.7

Accountants' Perceptions of the Communications Trap

Importance and frequency of communications	Important communications	Less-important communications
Received frequently	None	See if you have referrals to make
Received infrequently	Provide feedback on other clients who were referred	See if you have referrals to make; Announce new products and services; Stay in touch; Find out about changes in your practice; Do something personal; Tell you about changes in laws and regulations; Discuss new incentives for referrals; Tell you about new training opportunities they provide

from money managers, but all agree that they are not hearing frequently about what matters to them.

We can make our message a little clearer by consolidating the data we assembled above: charting the perceived frequency of communications against their felt importance. We have done this separately for each kind of advisor—insurance agents, accountants and attorneys. There can be no doubt that advisors feel many investment managers are doing a poor job in communicating with them. The "Communications Trap" graphics should make this plain [Tables 6.6, 6.7, 6.8]. The upper-left quadrant we reserve for important communications that are made frequently; it's empty for all three kinds of advisors.

Since advisors are definite about what communications are important to them, managers should be able to meet their desires—if they are willing to change their habits.

The first step in avoiding the communications trap is to identify what it is that the advisors in your network want. Start with the advisors you are in touch with most often, and the ones with whom you have the best relationships. You can also take guidance from the data in this book. Advisors want to know three main things from managers:

- How are previously referred high-net-worth clients doing? What is the status of the relationship with the investment manager? What services are being performed? How satisfied is the affluent client?

Table 6.8

Attorneys' Perceptions of the Communications Trap		
Importance and frequency of communications	Important communications	Less-important communications
Received frequently	None	See if you have referrals to make
Received infrequently	Tell about new training opportunities they provide; Provide feedback on other clients who were referred	Announce new products and services; Stay in touch; Find out about changes in your practice; Do something personal; Tell you about changes in laws and regulations; Discuss new incentives for referrals

- Are there new events or resources that would be helpful in building skills and capacities?
- Are there new business development plans or programs such as reciprocal referrals (or compensations for agents), joint marketing programs or the like?

Proactivity

Clearly, communicating frequently on the matters important to an advisor will make your referring relationship more productive. But there's more to it than that. Who initiates the communication affects the whole tenor of the relationship. One of the greatest mistakes any manager can make is to

Table 6.9

Percent of Advisors Who Say They Frequently Contact the Investment Manager in Order to...

	Insurance Agents	Accountants	Attorneys
Find out about new incentives for referrals	26.0%	0.0%	0.0%
Do something of a personal nature (e.g., birthday card, holiday gift)	25.0%	0.0%	0.0%
Find out how they handle referrals	24.5%	2.3%	0.0%
Obtain feedback on other clients you have referred	17.0%	26.4%	123.6%
See if they have referrals to make to you	10.0%	38.5%	42.2%
"Stay in touch" for other reasons	4.5%	12.6%	11.1%
Find out about new training opportunities they provide	2.5%	1.7%	6.0%
Learn about changes in your practice and clients	1.0%	1.1%	1.0%
Announce new products and services you have available	0.5%	0.0%	1.0%
Find out about changes in laws and regulations that might affect your clients	0.0%	0.0%	7.0%

be passive in his/her communications with referring advisors. Of course, it is easy to forget to keep advisors in the loop with the press of other priorities. But the passivity trap is the business-eroding trap. Other managers are competing for referrals from the same advisors. Advisors respond positively to the proactive manager—the manager who keeps them in the loop.

Unfortunately, many managers do not do this. Advisors often feel they have to do all the work. Specifically, they feel they are the ones who have to initiate contacts with investment managers to satisfy their information needs. This is what we examine in this section.

We started by looking at a range of reasons for communicating (similar to those of the previous section), but this time we asked advisors if they frequently initiated contact with investment managers for these reasons. Not surprisingly, we found that the leading reasons for which advisors call managers involve compensation or business-building possibilities (i.e., new incentives for insurance agents, and referrals for the advisor, attorneys and accountants). Accountants and attorneys also call for such reasons as getting feedback on previously referred clients (an important issue to them) and "staying in touch." Feedback on referred clients is of interest to insurance agents, who also call to do things of a personal nature and to find out how the manager handles referrals [Table 6.9].

The data in the table shows that the concerns that prompt accountants and attorneys to get in touch with investment managers are fairly similar; insurance agents have their own set of reasons motivating communication. It is essential for money managers to keep track of the communication needs of all advisors and do their best to meet them proactively.

Part of keeping abreast of the information needs of advisors is learning how they (advisors) routinely obtain information about high-net-worth client satisfaction and client-investment manager relations. Basically, there are two primary sources of data—the investment manager and the affluent client. And there are two basic approaches. One is proactive, in which the advisor seeks out feedback on the events following the referral. The other is reactive, in which the advisor awaits feedback spontaneously provided by the investment manager or the high-net-worth client.

We found substantial differences among the types of advisor when we looked at what was going on in this area [Table 6.10]. Insurance agents get their information from the investment manager much more often than they do from the client. Accountants and attorneys are more client-focused—they are far more likely to talk about what is going on with the client than with the manager. Accountants use both proactive and reactive methods—they actively ask the client and they also receive communications from the client. Attorneys tend to be reactive—to wait for the client to bring up concerns.

This data on how advisors seek out information about their referrals

Table 6.10

	Communications Dynamics—Advisors		
	Insurance Agents	Accountants	Attorneys
Ask the investment manager to find out what is going on	69.5%	10.4%	11.1%
The investment manager tells advisor	60.0%	33.3%	18.6%
Ask the client to find out what is going on	30.2%	76.9%	24.6%
The client tells advisor	27.0%	75.9%	58.3%

are brought into high relief when you look at the actual frequency of contacts between investment managers and advisors [Table 6.11]. The overall frequency of contacts is low, and the proportion initiated by advisors is all too high.

Given the volume of referrals some insurance agents make over the course of a year, the infrequency of contact between them and investment managers is striking. Almost half of all referring agents (49.5%) say they have not received a single contact from the investment manager to whom they made their most recent referral in the past year. As you might expect, if agents don't hear from a manager, they get concerned. They wonder about the high-net-worth client and fear that problems have come up. In order to put their fears to rest, agents will initiate contact if they haven't heard from a manager in a while. All agents say they had to initiate at least one contact in the past twelve months with the investment manager to whom they made their most recent referral.

Accountants are somewhat more likely to feel that investment managers stay in touch with them [Table 6.12]. Just about all accountants say they had at least one interaction initiated by the investment manager and many had one per quarter or more (59.8%). Investment managers typically initiate from three to more than 20 contacts a year. This level of interaction is apparently satisfactory to accountants; most (66.6%) say they initiate, at most, two contacts on their own initiative. Thus when contacts from investment managers are considered with contacts to investment managers, it would appear that communications between investment managers and accountants are a routine occurrence, with at least one interaction a quarter or more being the norm.

Table 6.11

Number of Update Calls For Agents in the Past Year

	Manager called agent	Agent had to call manager
Never	49.5%	0.0%
1 to 2 times	20.5%	52.0%
3 to 5 times	5.5%	23.5%
6 to 10	7.0%	14.5%
11 to 15	10.0%	6.0%
16 to 20	5.0%	2.5%
More than 20 times	2.5%	1.5%

All attorneys say they had at least one interaction initiated by the investment manager and that they initiated one or more such contact [Table 6.13]. Investment managers typically initiate from three to 15 contacts a year. Almost half (46.7%) of attorneys say they initiated three to five contacts themselves. Counting contacts initiated by both parties, it would appear that communication between investment managers and attorneys is a routine occurrence, with at least one interaction a month

Table 6.12

Number of Update Calls For Accountants in the Past Year

	Manager called accountant	Accountant had to call manager
None	1.7%	6.3%
1 to 2 times	38.5%	60.3%
3 to 5 times	21.3%	14.4%
6 to 10	23.0%	7.5%
11 to 15	8.0%	7.5%
16 to 20	4.6%	4.0%
More than 20 times	2.9%	0.0%

being the norm.

The frequency and content (and thus to a large degree the quality) of communications are under the direct control of investment managers; there's no reason to accept poor performance in these areas.

Advisors are extremely client-oriented and have a great need to stay abreast of client needs and experiences. In many ways this need is not being met at present, so opportunities exist for investment managers who can create superior communications programs with their referring advisors and be able to reassure them on the issue of trust. Such programs should include:

- Frequent and detailed information on all high-net-worth clients referred by the advisor;
- Behavior designed to reassure advisors the manager is trustworthy; personal gestures, cross-referrals, prompt announcements of upcoming seminars and new services, and
- Messages and behaviors designed to reinforce the intention to create a mutually beneficial long-term relationship.

Relationships

When there are significant and costly consequences to switching from one relationship to another, people will generally invest in the relationship. They do so to lower their long-term costs and risks. The relationships between advisors and managers can involve high switching costs. Advisors who are comfortable with the investment managers to whom they refer

Table 6.13

Number of Update Calls For Attorneys in the Past Year		
	Manager called attorney	Attorney had to call manager
Never	0.0%	0.0%
1 to 2 times	2.0%	17.6%
3 to 5 times	32.7%	46.7%
6 to 10	28.1%	21.6%
11 to 15	25.1%	8.5%
16 to 20	8.5%	4.5%
More than 20 times	3.5%	1.0%

tend to stay with them; dissatisfied advisors, on the other hand, are quite willing to try out new managers if they see a possible basis of trust.

All this would seem to make it clear that it is very much in the interest of managers to do all they can to enhance the quality of their existing relationships with advisors and make it as clear as possible that they are committed to long-term mutually rewarding associations. Presumably, most money managers would say that is just what they do. But when we asked advisors to assess the quality of their relationships with investment managers, we find they are not greatly impressed.

With insurance agents, the bottom line is that they are highly rational and self-interested. If they can find managers as interested in serving the client as they are, they will stop spreading their referrals around and concentrate them on that investment manager. As we have seen, there are ways managers can build their share by investing in relationships with advisors. But only a fairly small number of insurance agents (27.5%) say that managers have shown a desire for a long-term relationship with their referring agents, and fewer still (19.5%) say the investment manager provides marketing or technical information that could help agents improve their business [Table 6.14]. Only compensation seems to be well regarded, with a majority of agents believing compensation levels are appropriate and fair.

When it comes to accountants, we have seen how they distribute referrals among investment managers. It is in the accountant's interest to sustain the market relationship with investment managers to whom they routinely refer, and the same holds true for investment managers. Accountants who become adept at referring, as almost all do, can generate referrals on the average of more than one a month. This is an extremely attractive, and cost-effective, source of new referrals.

Accountants, however, do not generally feel as though they are part of a long-term, mutually beneficial relationship with investment managers. Few report that the investment managers they work with have expressed the desire to develop a long-term relationship (20.1%), shown that they have a willingness to help even if there is nothing in it for them (19.5%), or taken the other steps that help build trust and relationships.

Attorneys are somewhat more likely than accountants and insurance agents to feel that investment managers are avowedly eager for long-term relationships and ready to offer help even when deriving no immediate benefit. Still, more than half of the attorneys we surveyed did not give investment managers the nod on these or any other index of relationship quality.

In one sense, the data assembled on the chart is not encouraging: clearly, investment managers do not impress advisors in the arena of relationships. But this general low level of accomplishment means that great success can be achieved by managers who create and deploy programs designed to increase the satisfaction of referring advisors. Each manager will design a program tailored to their practice and client base, but the most successful programs will incorporate many of the keys to satisfaction discussed here.

To be sure their efforts are paying off, investment managers should track referrals, by advisor, over time. Investment managers should also track individual advisor satisfaction over time, by keeping in touch with them. This will insure they capture the greatest volume of referrals possible.

The initiatives and approaches we have discussed should enable

Table 6.14

Advisors' Assessments of Relationship Quality			
	Insurance Agents	Accountants	Attorneys
The money management firm has expressed a willingness to help even if there is nothing in it for them.	14.5%	19.5%	43.7%
The money management expressed the desire to develop a long-term relationship.	27.5%	20.1%	42.7%
You feel treated the same as someone who has made five times the number of referrals you have.	12.5%	16.7%	42.7%
The marketing or technical information provided by the investment manager enables you to improve your business with affluent clients.	19.5%	15.5%	40.2%
The investment manager's compensation to you is appropriate and fair.	69.1%	0.0%	39.1%
The investment manager does a good job of providing you with referrals.	5.0%	16.2%	7.5%
The money management firm asks your advice on client matters.	0.0%	7.5%	1.0%

investment managers to create an advisor referral network that will produce results. But we cannot stress too often the need to act consistently in implementing a marketing program geared to cultivating advisors.

All too often, investment managers do something very right and then fail to carry on with their efforts. We believe the findings we have reported here emphasize the importance of consistency and proactivity. We have also been able to identify many specific actions investment managers can take to create higher degrees of trust in the relationships, starting with more frequent, and appropriate, communications to the advisors who refer to them.

In the end, investment managers must realize that the answer to creating enduring relationships with advisors is to help them in appropriate ways. For insurance agents, it is with some form of compensation. For accountants and attorneys, it is by taking care of the high-net-worth client, joint marketing and increasing the volume of cross-referrals. Doing these things—doing them consistently—will take you far on the path to success in building an investment management business for high-net-worth clients.